STO

VGM Opportunities Series

OPPORTUNITIES IN STATE AND LOCAL GOVERNMENT CAREERS

Neale Baxter
Revised by
Hope M. Rajala

Foreword by
Governor James R. Thompson
State of Illinois, 1977–1991

VGM Career Horizons
a division of *NTC Publishing Group*
Lincolnwood, Illinois USA

Cover Photo Credits

Front cover: upper left, American
Petroleum Institute; upper right,
Cedarville College; lower left,
Waste Age; lower right, San Francisco
Police Department.

Back cover: upper left, Evanston
Police Department; upper right,
VISTA; lower left, Milwaukee County
Park Commission.

Library of Congress Cataloging-in-Publication Data

Baxter, Neale.
   Opportunities in state and local government careers/Neale Baxter
   revised by   ; forword by.

      p.   cm.—(VGM opportunities series)
   Includes bibliographical references.
   ISBN 0–8442–4040–0   ISBN 0–8442–4041–9 (pbk.)
   1. Civil service positions—United States—States. 2. Local
government—Vocational guidance—United States. I. Title.
II. Series.
   JK2465.B39 1985B
   353.9'3103—dc20   92–14629
                                                    CIP

Published by VGM Career Horizons, a division of NTC Publishing Group.
© 1993 by NTC Publishing Group, 4255 West Touhy Avenue,
Lincolnwood (Chicago), Illinois 60646-1975 U.S.A.

2 3 4 5 6 7 8 9 0 VP 9 8 7 6 5 4 3 2 1

ABOUT THE AUTHOR

Neale Baxter is managing editor of *The Occupational Outlook Quarterly*, a general career information magazine published by the U.S. Department of Labor. He has also served with the U.S. Army overseas and worked for state and local governments. He has written for *Career World* and the *Monthly Labor Review*, and teaches at George Mason University.

Mr. Baxter received his bachelor's degree from Manhattan College, his master's from Purdue University, and his Ph.D. from the University of North Carolina at Chapel Hill. He lives in Virginia with his wife and two children.

FOREWORD

Choosing a career is an important and highly personal decision. It can be difficult to find a field that offers the diversity needed for personal and professional satisfaction, while providing the security of a permanent job market.

One field which offers both security and satisfaction is public service. This book, Neale Baxter's *Opportunities in State and Local Government Careers,* will help you learn more about the challenges and rewards of a career in public service. Part of the VGM Career Horizons Series, Mr. Baxter's book outlines dozens of interesting careers available in our state and local governments.

My career in public service has spanned over thirty years. I have seen government operate at the local level as an assistant county prosecutor, and at the state level as governor of the nation's sixth-largest state. Throughout my career, the thing which has given me the greatest sense of pride and accomplishment is opening the doors of government to talented young people. Government affects each of us daily in many ways. Because it is such a crucial element of modern life, it is essential that our young people consider public service as a way to gain invaluable experience while making a vital positive impact on the community.

Serving the citizens of Illinois as governor gave me a sense of satisfaction unmatched by any other in my career. Actually seeing your ideas and decisions enhance the quality of life for others is the greatest benefit of a career in public service.

I hope you find the public service field to be as fascinating as I did. If so, this book will provide you with the information you need to embark on a career in state or local government. If making a difference in your world means more to you than merely getting a job, I can assure you that you are well on your way to a satisfying career. Good luck!

Governor James R. Thompson
State of Illinois, 1977–1991

CONTENTS

CHAPTER 1

WHO IS THIS BOOK FOR?

Teacher, police officer, librarian, social worker—if you wish to enter one of these occupations, this book is for you, because most of these workers are employed by state and local governments.

Nurse, word processor, accountant, civil engineer—if you wish to follow one of these occupations, this book is for you, too, because state and local governments employ thousands of these workers.

State and local governments are major providers of *services*. They provide education, mass transportation, fire protection, health services, and welfare services. Consequently, they are likely employers for people in the following occupations:

Accountant
Building Engineer
Building Inspector
Computer Programmer, Analyst
Coach
College and University
    Instructor
Emergency Medical Technician
Extension Service Specialist
Firefighter
Food Service Worker
Forester
Health Inspector
Highway Maintenance Worker

Land Use Manager
Librarian
Nutritionist
Police Officer
Sanitation Worker
School Principal
Sheriff
Teacher
Urban and Regional Planner
Water and Wastewater
    Conservation and Treatment
    Worker
Word Processor

1

These governments also employ more people *in their own operations* than any other industry in the country. As a consequence, thousands of people in the following occupations work for them:

Administrative Assistant	Guard
Accounting Clerk	Heavy Equipment Operator
Automotive Mechanic	Lawyer
Bookkeeper	Licensed Practical Nurse
Building Engineer	Maintenance Worker
Civil Engineer	Nursing Aide and Orderly
Clerical Supervisor	Physician
Clinical Lab Technician	Psychiatric Aide
Computer Programmer	Recreation Worker
Electrician	Registered Nurse
File Clerk	Social Worker
Food Services Worker	Systems Analyst
Gardener and Groundskeeper	Therapist

Altogether, more than 14.4 million people work for these governments, which means that they account for one job in eight. This book is a guide to these jobs. It will introduce you to the scope of state and local government and point out the incentives and drawbacks of a government career.

The book also describes hiring procedures and provides tips on filling out applications, taking physical and aptitude tests, handling interviews, and finding jobs.

Much of the book deals with specific occupations in which governments are either the major employer or the employer of thousands of workers; more than 78 percent of all state and local government employees are in these occupations. In addition, many small occupations associated with state and local government—city manager, for example—are described. For each of the major occupations, there is information on the nature of the work, what you should bring to the occupation, its rewards, where you can get a job, and where to learn more about the field. For other occupations, at least some information is given on the nature of the work, training required, number of people employed, and—usually—sources of information besides those listed in the appendix material.

The section on *the nature of the work,* which immediately follows the occupation's title, describes the usual duties and work environment of the job, including information on unusual work hours or working conditions.

"What you should bring to this occupation" describes the personal characteristics, aptitudes, skills, experience, and education that make people successful at this kind of work. The kinds of tests applicants must usually take are also indicated, along with the training given to new workers.

"The rewards" deals with salaries and other benefits, such as vacation and sick leaves; it also indicates nonmonetary benefits, such as personal satisfaction or the chances for advancement, and some things to make you think twice about the occupation—the reasons why some workers are dissatisfied.

"Where to find a job" indicates the number of people who work for state and local governments in this occupation, mentioning the usual employing agency when possible. Other sources of employment are also given for many occupations. Information on the job outlook over the next ten years is also given, in cases where projections are available.

The last section, *"Where to learn more,"* provides the names and addresses of associations of workers in the field and lists periodicals and books that can give you more insight into the occupation. The sources of information listed in the appendix material should also prove useful.

CHAPTER 2

THOUSANDS OF EMPLOYERS, MILLIONS OF JOBS

Let's begin with the scope of state and local government—its size and major functions.

By any measure, government employment is very large. About 4.2 million people worked for the states in 1988 and 10.2 million worked for local governments, a total of over 14.4 million. That's a pretty large number to imagine. It equals the population of the entire country in 1830, and is more than the population of all but the three largest states today. You could spend $100,000 a year for the rest of your life and not run through half that many dollars.

The size of the state and local government labor force varies from place to place, ranging from almost one and a half million workers in California to less than 29,000 in Vermont. Population is the major reason for the differences, but many other factors also come into play. Some variation is due to different needs. Rural areas don't need the same services that large cities do; and if the private sector traditionally provides hospitals or utilities, the state or local government does not have to. But much of the variation is also due to the willingness and ability of the citizens to pay for government services.

One way to look at government employment besides the total number of people working is the number of state and local workers per 10,000 citizens. The average is 490, but even here, there is much variation, ranging from 725 in Alaska to 398 in Pennsylvania. Other states with high employment to population ratios are Wyoming, Nebraska, New

Mexico, and New York; other states with low ratios include New Hampshire, Ohio, Illinois, and Indiana.

The employment-population ratio also varies from function to function within a state. For example, the ratio for Georgia hospitals is very high, but it's a little below average in parks and recreation. Nevada has a low ratio in education and a very high one in correction.

STEADY GROWTH

Government employment experienced rapid and sustained growth from World War II to 1980. Although we tend to associate government with the national scene, the growth was not at the federal level, which has never regained its wartime peak. Instead, the increasing employment was at the state and local levels, where the labor force grew an average of 3 percent a year from 1945 to 1980. For state governments, which generally grew faster than local governments, much of the increase was for higher education, hospitals, public welfare, general control, health, and correction. Local governments added on workers in elementary and secondary education, higher education, hospitals, police protection, general control, public transit, health, and public welfare.

In 1980, government employment reached a peak. The next year, the number of state and local government workers fell for the first time since World War II. Some decline occurred in almost every function except police protection. Education—which represents so much of the total— had the greatest loss in numbers; highway departments had the sharpest percentage drop. The total decline was 245,000, almost all of which was at the state and local levels which fell 1.8 percent.

Employment rose again in 1983, reaching 13,159,000. The upward trend reached 14.4 million in 1988 and is likely to continue, though state and local employment opportunities are not projected to grow as fast as the rest of the economy in the the near future. Besides hiring workers for new jobs, these employers will be hiring huge numbers of workers to replace those currently employed who go to work for private firms, retire, or leave the labor force for some other reason. A turnover rate of about 10 percent is fairly common; given the size of the government labor force, that means that more than one million jobs would open up in government service each year. By comparison, all the workers of the nation's two largest corporations in terms of employment now number about one million.

WHAT DO ALL THESE PEOPLE DO?

Given these millions of workers, you might expect to be hard pressed to answer the question, "What do all these people do?" But the answer is surprisingly easy for almost half of them—they educate us. Education accounts for far more jobs than any other government function. Local governments—usually special school districts—are the major employers of people who work in education, including teachers, administrators, teacher aides, librarians, and school counselors. Other major functions of local governments are providing police and fire protection, hospitals, streets and highways, water, and transit service.

Employees of state governments are not quite as concentrated *by field* as local government workers are, although 30 percent are engaged in higher education. Functions employing at least 5 percent of all state workers are hospitals, highways, correction, and public welfare. This means that state governments employ many college professors, librarians, nurses, psychiatric aides, other medical specialists, engineers, highway construction workers, correction officers or prison guards, social workers, and welfare aides.

As you can see, government is a very large industry. But that does not make finding a job easy, primarily because there are so many different employers: 50 states plus 5 territories, Puerto Rico, and the District of Columbia; approximately 3,000 counties; 19,200 municipalities; 16,700 towns; 29,600 special districts; and, finally, 14,700 school districts.

That makes 83,000 different governments, or governmental bodies each of which does its own hiring. And each government may have more than one hiring system. Each state, for example, has an agency similar to the former Civil Service Commission of the federal government that establishes eligibility standards, administers examinations, and maintains registers of eligible applicants. But as many of half the state's employees may be hired according to other procedures. For example, the court system and the legislature are not usually under the civil service system.

Despite the existence of these many different systems, all is not chaos. As shown in the following chapter, many of the benefits and even the disadvantages of government employment are roughly comparable. And many governments follow the same kinds of hiring procedures. Besides, with 83,000 potential employers, you have that many more places to find a job.

FOR WHAT KINDS OF GOVERNMENTS?

State and local governments come in more shapes and sizes than blue jeans. The U. S. Census Bureau conducts an annual survey of government employment. For the survey, it divides governments among the following groups.

- *County.* Organized county governments, called *boroughs* in Alaska and *parishes* in Louisiana.
- *Municipality.* A political subdivision of a county that provides general government services to a concentrated population in a defined geographic area. Municipalities are also called cities, villages, boroughs (except in Alaska), and towns (except in New England, Minnesota, New York, and Wisconsin). Some municipalities have taken over the entire area of a county or, in the case of New York City, several counties. Among these cities are Anaconda; Anchorage; Baltimore; Baton Rouge; Boston; Butte; Carson City; Columbus, Georgia; Denver; Honolulu; Indianapolis; Jacksonville; Juneau; Lexington, Kentucky; Nashville; New Orleans; Philadelphia; St. Louis; Sitka; and San Francisco. Washington, DC, combines the functions of a city, county, and state government.
- *Township.* A subdivision of a county that provides general government services in a defined geographical area without regard to the concentration of the population. Twenty states use this classification. The governments are called *towns* in New England, New

York, and Wisconsin; *plantations* in Maine; and *locations* in New Hampshire.

- *School District.* Census notes that "There is a marked organizational diversity in the types of governmental units that provide for the operation of public schools." School districts that are completely independent of all other local governments are found in 45 states. Dependent school systems are found in Alaska, Hawaii, Maryland, North Carolina, Virginia, and Washington, DC; the school system is dependent on a local government or the state government. Eleven states have both independent and dependent school systems.
- *Special District.* A government that provides only one or a few related services, which makes them like school districts. The district may be called an authority, board, or commission. Among the services provided by special districts are soil conservation, water, bridges, housing, community development, fire protection, and hospitals. These districts, like school districts, vary enormously in size.

LOOK AT THE PAST AND AT THE FUTURE

We can see by examining Table 1 that the trend since 1942 has been to fewer and fewer units of state and local government. This trend is most noticeable in the totals for school districts. The decades of the 1940s and 1950s saw a rapid decline in rural and small town districts as people began to recognize the need for broader education programs to meet the challenges of a technological society. The only significant increase has been in the number of special districts. As the table shows, the total overall is rising again.

The decline in the number of units of state and local government does not, however, tell the story of public sector employment. During the years from 1950–1990, the number of employees more than tripled in local governmental units and quadrupled at the state level. See Table 2.

The shifts in both the number of units of state and local governments and the number of citizens employed in the public sector can be traced

Table 1

TRENDS IN STATE AND LOCAL GOVERNMENT EMPLOYMENT NUMBER OF *UNITS* OF GOVERNMENT			
	1942	*1962*	*1982*
States	48	50	50
Local			
County	3,050	3,043	3,041
Municipal	16,220	16,778	19,076
Town/Township	18,919	17,202	16,734
School	108,579	67,346	14,851
Special	8,299	12,319	28,588
TOTAL	155,067	116,688	82,290*

*By 1990 this figure was 83,236.

Table 2

STATE AND LOCAL EMPLOYMENT 1950–1990 (by 1,000s)			
	1950	*1970*	*1990*
State	1,057	2,755	4,231
Local	3,228	7,392	10,240*
*County	1,985,000		
Municipal	2,657,000		
Town/Township	416,000		
School	4,614,000		
Special District	568,000		

to several factors. First, the increase in population of the United States—from 151,326,000 in 1950 to 248,709,000 in 1990—producing greater needs for all services. Second, greater expectations and demands for social services. Third, a trend to return tax monies to the states rather than continuing federal programs (revenue sharing, block grants, etc.). In 1960, the federal government returned 7 billion to the states—by 1986 that figure reached 86 billion.

The future appears to hold a very small, but steady growth in the number of units of state and local government—mostly in the category of special districts. We can also look forward to a steady, if not dramatic, increase in the number of employment opportunities in public service.

AND HOW ARE THE GOVERNMENTS ORGANIZED?

Some governments closely follow the federal organization, that is all executive functions are directed by a mayor or governor just as the President is in charge of all departments of the national government. More frequently, however, the chief executive does *not* control all departments. In addition to a governor, many states elect an attorney general, commissioner of education, and other officials, each of whom has final authority for a department; this is sometimes referred to as the plural executive system of government. At the local level, legislative and executive functions are often invested in a single body, the board, which makes local government very different from the federal model. Most local governments follow one of four patterns.

- *Mayor-council or elected executive-council:* these governments do resemble the federal system.
- *Council-city manager or commission-county manager:* the council acts as the legislature and hires a professional manager to see to day-to-day administration. The council may also choose a mayor from among its members, but the office is largely ceremonial.
- *Commissioner:* the commissioners as a group exercise legislative functions; each commissioner is also the head of one or more departments; a major or chief administrative officer may be elected separately or chosen by the board from among its members.
- *Town Meeting:* a meeting of the electorate or a large number of elected representatives sets policy and chooses a board of selectmen to carry the policies out; the meeting or the board may also hire a professional manager.

CHAPTER 3

REWARDS AND FRUSTRATIONS OF GOVERNMENT EMPLOYMENT

The benefits and drawbacks of government employment largely depend on the particular occupation you enter or the individual job you hold. The satisfactions of a teacher, for example, are very different from those of a police officer. Still and all, some of the pluses and minuses of a government job hold true across many occupations.

EARNINGS

Generalizing about the pay practices of thousands of different employers is risky. Studies show that one government pays its clerical workers relatively well while its electricians would do better with a private company; another government does just the opposite, paying electricians much better than average and clerical workers less than the going rate. After studying many surveys of government versus private sector wages, Shawna Grosskopf concludes, "Roughly speaking, high-skill occupations are relatively underpaid in the public sector, and low-skill occupations are overpaid relative to the private sector." That does not mean, however, that you can assume a particular government job pays better or worse than one with a private firm.

When asking about salaries, people often request a figure, but they really want to know how one occupation's salary compares with another's. Here are some occupations and average 1990 salaries.

Civil Engineer	$35,200
Computer Programmer	30,600
Accountant	29,500
Police Officer	26,700
Firefighter	25,500
Teacher (secondary level)	30,300
Registered Nurse	32,100
Teacher (elementary level)	28,900
Administrative Assistant	21,700
Typist/Word Processor	18,100
Nurse's Aide	12,000
Physician Assistant	29,600

In 1990 the median income for all workers was $28,000. Besides putting salary information into a context, comparisons have the advantage of remaining accurate for a longer period. Changes in economic conditions quickly make salary figures out of date, but the relative salaries for different occupations remain more constant. You can use this information when you are offered a salary to help you evaluate the proposal. Here are some considerations to keep in mind in addition to dollar amounts.

- What do private companies pay workers in the occupation? Even if government pays a little less, the other benefits and the security of a government position may make it worthwhile to consider.
- Is the 'annual' salary paid in less than 12 months—as in the case of many teachers? If so, you can correct for distortion.
- Besides salary, do you receive benefits such as housing or meals that lower your cost of living?
- Is the occupation unionized? Union workers tend to be better paid, but they must also pay union dues.

Despite the great number of employers and the many different occupations involved, many government and private-sector employees enjoy comparable fringe benefits. The most common are paid vacation and sick leave, paid holidays, medical insurance, retirement plans, and tuition assistance. Comprehensive data are not available for local governments. However, the practices of the states show the usual benefits offered.

New workers typically get 2 weeks of vacation and 12 to 18 days of sick leave; almost all the states give additional vacation time to workers with more service; 25 or more days a year is the maximum in several states. Most states grant at least 8 paid holidays a year, and many have up to 12 or 13; Hawaii gives 15. The entire cost of medical insurance is paid in 14 states; 21 pay for life insurance. The rest of the states pay at least part of the cost of medical insurance and offer some kind of life insurance plan.

Government pensions are often considered generous. Florida, Mississippi, and Oklahoma pay the entire cost of the pension. In the rest of the states, the employer contributes to a pension fund, and the worker pays the balance.

Almost all the states provide tuition assistance for college. The amount provided and the kinds of courses that may be taken vary widely.

Other frequently mentioned benefits of government jobs are job security and advancement opportunities. Government employment is not guaranteed in bad times, as the teachers in many a shrinking school district can attest. Still, a government is less likely to be affected by temporary economic setbacks than is a private company. This side effect of government employment is especially beneficial in occupations that are prone to high unemployment, such as the construction crafts.

As for advancement, government positions often have clearly defined career ladders. Furthermore, in many government agencies, managerial positions are usually held by people who once worked at lower levels of the organization. For example, school administrators are often former teachers in the system; police sergeants and officers almost always come from the patrol ranks.

DISADVANTAGES

Just as government service offers some solid advantages, it has some disadvantages. The degree to which they bother you is likely to depend on your own personality. One frustration of government work for some is the inability to measure achievement in terms of profit and loss. When a private company offers goods or services to the public, it can use sales to measure its success. Governments do not sell products on the open market, and government programs rarely have a clear-cut success. No matter how good the schools, no matter how safe the community, no matter how well kept the roads, some citizens will always be found to say that the service should be better or cheaper or both. Politics also has a major effect on government workers, since politicians control the budget and make the final decisions. This can be a disadvantage to those who always want to have the last word on their own work. Furthermore, the same organization controls that provide job security can protect the job of someone you feel you should replace. And the explicit promotion procedures can result in advancement that is sure but slow. Nor does the government offer the extremely high salaries and bonuses that a few very successful workers in the private sector make.

Most of these drawbacks are not unique to the government; they are shared by many large organizations. And perhaps they all amount to saying nothing more than that people who enjoy the risks and rewards of self-employment will find less satisfaction working for the government. They are worth considering, however, before you decide to build a government career.

AND THE MAJOR REWARD

The economic benefits of government employment may or may not outweigh the drawbacks. For millions of government employees, however, the equation is not between the money you get and the hassles you go through. The reward isn't in the paycheck; it's in the people you help. These jobs are sometimes referred to as public service. The rewards of public service are in the good that is accomplished, the ignorance that is corrected, the sickness that is healed, and the fears that are comforted. The major benefits of government employment are intangible—most importantly, the opportunity to serve the public good and have a direct impact on other people. As a government official, social worker, teacher, police officer, or fire fighter, you will be able to see how your work benefits individuals and the community at large.

CHAPTER 4

HIRING PROCEDURES

One of your first tasks if you seek a particular government job is to learn what hiring procedures are used to fill it. For some jobs, you must be elected. For others, you are appointed by an elected official who has a free hand, subject to review by the board or legislature. These jobs are usually for a limited term; often, you lose your job if the person who appointed you is not reelected. These elected and appointed positions are the stuff of local politics. In general, a person who decides on policies is likely to hold one of them.

Most government workers are neither elected nor appointed in this way, however. They are appointed, or hired, according to some kind of merit or civil service system. Usually, they keep their jobs without regard to political events. People who put government policy into action are likely to be hired in accordance with a merit system.

For any given occupation, most governments pretty much use the same procedure. Mayors and sheriffs, for example, are almost always elected. City managers and police chiefs are appointed. Police officers must qualify by a series of tests. Teachers are selected by educational standards. Of course, one government will sometimes follow a different procedure for a particular occupation. School board members, for example, are elected in much of the country, but they are appointed in Virginia. And some jobs in one occupation might be handled differently than most. Secretary is usually a merit position, but the mayor's secretary, or administrative assistant, is likely to be appointed.

MERIT SYSTEMS

Merit systems are used by all the states and most large city and county governments for at least some positions. The larger a government is, the more likely it is to have a merit system, which is why the vast majority of government jobs are covered by such systems even though only a bare majority of governments use them.

Under a merit system, the duties of people in a given job are clearly defined. And the qualifications required of someone who can hold that job are also spelled out in detail. All applicants for a position must be ranked according to their skills and training; the position must then be offered to one of the most highly ranked applicants.

Note that the job need not go to the highest ranked individual, just one of the highest ranked. The person doing the hiring, therefore, has some leeway in reaching a final decision. A school principal, for example, often has the last word with regard to a new teacher, and a program manager can usually hire any one of several qualified applicants. This leeway is why you must actively hunt for a government job, as explained in the next chapter, and not just wait for your name to come to the top of a list. People are more likely to hire someone who has contacted them than someone who is only a name on a piece of paper.

The nuts and bolts of a merit system differ from one government to another. But in all of them, when an agency—be it a school, a police department, or a hospital—needs to hire someone, it usually issues an announcement of some kind indicating that workers are sought in one occupation or another.

THE REAL WORLD

In an ideal world, all applicants for employment in either the private or public sector would be treated equally and judged solely on the basis of test performance and a well-structured interview. We all know, however, that in the real world vacancies in the private sector are often filled using such criteria as: family or friend recommendation, networking, political connections, and so on.

The public sector is not free from the same influences. While eventually the applicant must satisfactorily complete the more formal application requirements for a job, other factors will affect who gets the position. And this is not all to the bad. The person doing the hiring is, above all, interested in filling the vacancy with someone of good character, with satisfactory work habits, and with a stable lifestyle who will fit in well with the other people in the workplace. If that hirer consistently chooses people who leave after a short time, miss a number of workdays, or cause trouble with other employees, he or she will soon lose the authority to hire. He or she may also lose opportunities for career advancement on the grounds of poor judgment—or worse.

In his excellent book *The Complete Guide to Public Employment,* Dr. Ronald L. Krannich suggests that as many as 70 percent of high-level government vacancies may be somewhat less than fully open and competitive. He terms the widespread use of an unfair tactic in filling vacancies "wiring." This is a system of informally preselecting candidates and then writing a job description that is guaranteed to make them the best qualified for the job. He suggests that the practice may be unethical or unfair, but it is not illegal. It is, he says, ". . . business as usual. And it takes place in most units of government to some degree." Entry-level jobs are less likely to be affected by such practices, but even at that level you will want to do your best to make yourself more than just another properly filled out application form. A sincere recommendation from a friend already employed by a unit of state or local government will always be of benefit to you. Just be sure that your formal application will back up the informal help you get.

KINDS OF ANNOUNCEMENTS

Announcements can be a single page or a small booklet. Announcements almost always indicate the occupations being filled, their salary range, the qualifications required, the duties performed in the job, application procedures, and sources of more information.

Three different kinds of announcements are common.

- *Open announcement.* This means that applications are always accepted. Typically, this procedure is followed only for occupations with steady turnover, especially in the clerical field.
- *Announcement of an examination.* This means that applications are being accepted for evaluation or for a test; only after the evaluation will people be considered for actual job openings as they arise. (The methods used in evaluating applicants are described in the next chapter.)
- *Position announcement.* This means that applications are being accepted for a job that is currently available. In many cases, the people doing the hiring only consider applicants who have already been evaluated as a result of an announcement of an examination.

Note that you must often answer two announcements to find one job: First, an announcement of an examination, and, second, a position announcement. This means that *you can not look for a job on Friday and start work on Monday.* Even for clerical positions, where the need is constant and the evaluation process streamlined, you can easily spend from 3 to 6 months between the day you decide to look for a job and the day you start work. In many other occupations—such as police officer, fire fighter, and teacher—hiring takes place only once a year. If you miss the date on which applications to take a test are being accepted, you may have to wait an entire year before you can apply. The test itself may be some months later than the cut-off date for applications, and actual hiring may not take place for several months more. As a consequence, *three years* can pass between your decision to seek a job and your first paycheck. If you do miss the filing date, you'll at least have plenty of time to prepare for the test.

GENERAL REQUIREMENTS AND TYPES OF TESTS

Besides the specific qualifications for the job, applicants must usually meet some general requirements. United States citizenship is often required. Many state and local governments also prefer to hire residents as much as possible, but as a practical matter, they will hire otherwise qualified people for hard-to-fill jobs. For example, when librarians were hard to find during the 1960s, residency requirements were often ignored; they are now more often adhered to. According to John Zehrig in *Careers in State and Local Government,* only about half of all governments require residency.

Governments often—but not always—have a standard procedure to evaluate job applicants. The procedure is often called an examination, although no test might be given. The most frequently used evaluation procedures are the following:

- *Written tests.* Often multiple choice, samples of the tests are usually available from the government. Commercial publishers also sell books of sample tests for many occupations.
- *Performance tests.* Applicants for clerical and craft jobs must often show that they can operate the equipment or use the tools needed on the job.
- *Physical Agility.* Applicants for police, fire fighter, sanitation, or other positions that require specific levels of strength or agility must take tests designed to show that they can perform the same type of tasks as workers in the occupation.
- *Medical examinations.* Generally, applicants should be in good health. For some jobs, such as fire fighter, and police officer, standards are more rigorous than usual.
- *Ratings of education, training, and experience.* For many jobs, especially at the professional entry level, candidates are judged on the basis of the appropriateness of their education and experience to the occupation. An announcement that a government is accepting applications for such an evaluation should indicate the kind of education and experience sought. If you fill out such an application, it is your responsibility to make sure that your forms have all the needed information, even to the point of using the very words of the job description where appropriate. *Your rating depends exclusively on the evaluator's ability to find the required qualifications on your application.*
- *Interviews.* These are similar to the rating of education and experience described above. Interviews are used for occupations in which workers have frequent contact with the public, including police officer, fire fighter, and claims examiner.

- *All of the above.* For some jobs—police recruits and fire fighter recruits, for example—all these evaluation procedures are used.

In addition, many employers, both private and public, are requiring job applicants to sign affidavits that attest to the applicants' marital status, citizenship, and criminal record, if any. It is a mistake to attempt to conceal any facts about yourself through failing to be truthful. You will spend a lot of time and money and suffer the loss of your hopes and dreams if you are found out. If you lie, the chances are excellent that you *will* be found out. And, your signature on a false affidavit is all the grounds needed to terminate your employment. You will be better off if you are truthful, even if you must ask permission to explain the circumstances behind some of your responses. An arrest, long in the past, followed by years of good citizenship, may not be a problem. An alcohol problem followed by years of sobriety should not stigmatize you. Most people are fair-minded about mistakes from which others learned. If they are not, better to know that upfront and not six months or two years into a job you enjoy and don't want to lose.

In most cases, after you take a test or submit evidence of your education and experience, the personnel department rates you and notifies you of your rating. If you score highly enough, you are eligible for employment. Even a high rating is no guarantee of a job, however, and—as said above—your chances of employment are almost always improved if you go out and look for a position rather than wait for the personnel department to send your name to someone with a vacancy.

CHAPTER 5

HINTS ON RESUMES, APPLICATION FORMS, COVER LETTERS, TESTS, AND INTERVIEWS

When you envision this part of your job search, you might see a hurdle to leap over, or a hoop to jump through, or a barrier to knock down. That is how many people think of resumes, application forms, cover letters, tests, and interviews. But you do not have to think of them that way. They are not ways to keep you from a job; they are ways to you to show an employer how good you really are. After all, you are going to get a job. It is just a question of which one.

Governments, like other employers, want to hire people who can do the job. To learn who these people are, they use resumes, application forms, written tests, performance tests, medical examinations, and interviews. This chapter points out ways you can use all these different evaluation procedures to best advantage.

CREATING EFFECTIVE RESUMES AND APPLICATION FORMS

Resumes and application forms are two ways to achieve the same goal: to give the employer written evidence of your qualifications. When creating one, you need two different kinds of information: facts about yourself and facts about the job you want. You then present the facts about yourself in terms of the job. You have more freedom with a resume—you can put your best points first and avoid blanks. But even on application forms, you can describe your qualifications in terms of the job's duties.

WORK SHEETS

The best way to save your own time, and that of others, is to put together a work sheet that contains all the information you will need to draw up a basic resume—one that can be adapted for use in a variety of situations. More about that later. Your work sheet should also include any information that you might need when you have to fill out an application at the job site. You can guess the impression that is made by applicants who can't find their social security numbers or the addresses of former employers. Here are some things your work sheet should cover, but you will probably want to add others.

WORK SHEET INFORMATION

- Your current address and phone number. If you are hard to track down during business hours, also supply another number of someone reliable who will agree to take phone messages for you. You may also want to put down your last couple of addresses, particularly if you haven't been at your current address for a fairly long time.
- Your career goals, carefully thought out and edited to a concise paragraph. In a resume, you can wax a bit eloquent, but job application forms rarely give you much room for answers.
- Social security number.
- Experience (paid and volunteer)—complete with dates of employment, name and full address of employer, job title, starting and finishing salaries. You will also need to give your reason for leaving, and there are several that are acceptable—moving, returning to school, seeking a better position. If the circumstances of your leaving a job are unhappy, you may omit giving them, but be

prepared to answer truthfully, if asked. You may have been fired, but if that was because you refused to perform foolishly dangerous tasks, for example, it could even be a plus for you.

- Education—the last school you attended, its correct address, the years you attended, the diploma or degree you earned, and your major course of study.
- Other qualifications—special skills, hobbies, organizations you belong to, honors you have received. These activities often tell more about you as a person than do your work-for-pay activities.
- Office equipment, tools, machines you have used successfully.
- List of references. You will want four or five business and personal references. Be sure to get their permission to be approached. Supply correctly spelled names, current addresses, and telephone numbers. Indicate which are personal and which are business references.
- Some books will advise that you come right out and say the salary you expect to be paid. You may want to give a range that you find acceptable, or you may want to leave the matter open. Opportunities for advancement, geographic location, opportunities for travel may be of greater importance to you than a few dollars difference in salary at the beginning of your career. You don't want to limit your choices arbitrarily.
- Be frank about any disabilities you may have. Federal law protects your rights as a disabled person. Better you acknowledge your disability and then stress your *abilities* right from the start.
- If you have ever been convicted of a crime—admit it. You need not say anything about any charge of which you were acquitted.
- Finally, make several photocopies of your work sheet. If you fold it and carry it around to many places, it will soon become dog-eared and make it appear that you have been looking for work for several decades. Put one copy in a very safe place. After going through all of the hours it took to assemble your information, you don't want to have to start over!

Next, gather specific information about the jobs you are applying for. (The previous chapter discusses the announcements that usually contain this information for government jobs.) You need to know the pay range (so you won't ask for too much or too little), the education and experience usually required, hours and shifts usually worked. Most important, you need to know the job duties (so that you can describe your experience in terms of those duties). Study the job description; a government announcement might even have a checklist that assigns a numerical weight to different qualifications so that you can be certain as to which is the most important. If the announcement or ad is vague, call the agency to learn what is sought.

Once you have the information you need, you can prepare a resume. You may need to prepare more than one master resume if you are going to look for different kinds of jobs.

The way you arrange your resume depends on how well your experience seems to prepare you for the position you want. Basically, you can describe your most recent job first and work backwards (chronological resume); or group similar skills together (functional resume); or you can combine the two forms—as in the example provided. No matter which form you use, the following advice applies generally:

- *Use specifics.* A vague description of your duties will make only a vague impression.
- *Identify accomplishments.* If you improved productivity, reduced costs, increased membership, or achieved some other goal, say so.
- *Type your resume, using a standard typeface.* (Printed resumes are becoming more common, but employers do not indicate a preference for the use of fancy typefaces and design.
- *Keep the length down to two pages at the most.* (The sample in this chapter is a single page in its original format.)
- *Remember your mother's advice not to say anything if you can't say something nice.* Leave *all* embarrassing or negative information off the resume (but be ready to deal with it in a positive fashion at the interview).
- *Proofread the master copy carefully.*
- *Have someone else proofread the master copy carefully.*
- *Have a third person proofread the master copy carefully.*
- Use the best quality photocopying machine and good white or off-white paper.

SAMPLE RESUME

Emilie L. Baltz

<u>Address</u>
123 New Street
Anytown, CA 90210

<u>Telephone Number</u>
815-555-9248
(Another number,
    if needed)

Position sought: xxxxxxxxxxxxxxxxxxxxxxxxxxxxxxxx
xxxxxxxxxxxxxxxxxxxxxxxxxxxxxxxxxxxxxxxxxxxxxxxxxx
xxxxxxxxxxxxxxxxxxxxxxxxxxxxxxxxxxxxxxxxx.

EDUCATION
School, address, diploma or degree, year of completion.

COURSES RELEVANT TO POSITION
List those courses which add to desirability of applicant as
a future employee.

WORK EXPERIENCE
Start with your most recent employment experience and tell
specifically what your duties were and what you
accomplished in the situation. List both full and part-time
jobs.

VOLUNTEER OR EXTRACURRICULAR EXPERIENCE
Be specific about what you did with organizations—offices
held, honors awarded.

REFERENCES
List one or two business and personal references. Be
prepared to supply more, if required.

Government agencies typically make more use of *application forms* than of resumes. The forms suit the style of large organizations because people can find information more quickly if it always appears in the same place. *No matter how rigid the form appears to be, you can still use it to show why you are the person for the job being filled.*

At first glance, application forms seem to give a job hunter no leeway. The forms certainly do not have the the flexibility that a resume does, but you can use them to your best advantage. Remember that the attitude of the person reading the form is not "Let's find out why this person is unqualified," but "Maybe this is the person we want." Use all the parts of the form—experience blocks, education blocks, and others—to show that *the person is you.*

Here's some general advice on application forms:

- Request two copies of the form. If only one is provided, photocopy it before you make a mark on it. You'll need more than one copy to prepare rough drafts.
- Read the whole form before you start completing it.
- Prepare a master copy if the same form is used by several agencies. Do not fill in the specific job applied for, date, and signature on the master form. Fill in that information on the photocopies as you submit them.
- Type your entries on the application form if possible. If the form has lots of little lines that are hard to type within, ask if you can type the information on a piece of blank paper that will fit in the space, paste the paper over the form, and photocopy the finished product. Such a procedure results in a much neater, easier-to-read page.
- Leave no blanks; enter *n/a* (for "not applicable") when the information requested does not apply to you; this tells people checking the form that you did not simply skip the question.
- Carry a resume and a copy of other frequently-asked-for information (such as previous addresses) with you when visiting potential employers in case you must fill out an application on the spot. Whenever possible, however, fill the form out at home and mail it in with a resume and a cover letter that point up your strong points.

WRITING INTRIGUING COVER LETTERS

You will need a cover letter whenever you send a resume or application form to a potential employer. The letter should capture the employer's attention, show why you are writing, indicate why your employment will benefit the company, and ask for an interview.

Each letter should be addressed by name to the person you want to talk with. That person is the one who can hire you. This is almost certainly not someone in the personnel department, and it is probably not a department head either. It is most likely to be the person who will actually supervise you once you start work. Call the company to make sure you have the right name. And spell it correctly.

The opening should appeal to the reader. Cover letters are sales letters. Sales are made after you capture the person's attention. You capture someone's attention most easily by talking about them rather than yourself. Throughout this book, periodicals and associations that publish periodicals are listed. These periodicals can give you information you need to make the kind of personal tie-in that you are looking for, such as a special project that is underway. Other ways to catch the reader's eye besides mentioning projects under development are references to awards a person has recently received and favorable comments about the program that the person has run. If you are answering an ad, you can mention it. If someone that you know suggested that you write, use that person's name (with permission, of course).

The body of the letter gives a brief description of your qualifications, and refers to the resume, where your sales campaign can continue.

You cannot have what you do not ask for. Ask for an interview. Suggest a time. State that you will confirm the appointment.

Use a standard complementary close and signature block. Include a phone number—which is not yet part of a standard signature block, although it is found on most letterheads.

In order to be specific and relevant, each letter must be written individually. Each letter must also be typed perfectly. Word processing equipment can help. Frequently, only the address, first paragraph, and specifics concerning an interview will vary. These items are easily changed on word processing equipment and memory typewriters. If you

SAMPLE COVER LETTER

123 New Street
Anytown, CA 90210
September 24, 1992

Mr. John Christopher
Executive Director
Warren-Sharpe Community Center
472 South 21st Avenue
Allen, CA 90052

Dear Mr. Christopher:

Your announcement of a job opening at the Warren-Sharpe Community Center is of great interest to me.

I have six years of experience, both as a volunteer and as a part-time student worker, in programs similar to yours. In addition, I am fluent in the Spanish language, being a product of an American father and a mother who is a native of Haiti. I would, from the start, be able to communicate easily with the population you serve.

In addition, my college training has prepared me for a career in community social services. I have taken courses in sociology, psychology, social work, and recreational activities.

In my volunteer and part-time jobs I have worked with infants, assisting at a day-care center; coached track and volleyball; and acted as an ombudsman at a senior citizen housing center.

I believe I could bring the training and experience you are looking for to the job and am available for an interview at your convenience. My resume is enclosed, and I look forward to hearing from you.

Sincerely,

Emilie L. Baltz
815-555-9248

do not have access to such equipment, you might be able to rent it. Or you might be able to have your letters typed by a resume or employment service company. Two cautions are in order. First, as always, be sure you know the full cost of such a service. Second, many computer systems use dot-matrix printers; the resulting copy is not generally acceptable. If a service does your letters, be sure before you place the order that you will get letter-quality.

PASSING TESTS

A man with a violin case stood on a subway platform in the Bronx. He asked a conductor, "How do you get to Carnegie Hall?" The conductor replied, "Practice! Practice! Practice!"

That old joke holds good advice for test takers (and people preparing for interviews). The tests given to job applicants fall into four categories: general aptitude tests, practical tests, tests of physical agility, and medical examinations. You can practice for the first three. If the fourth is required, learn as soon as possible what the disqualifying conditions are, then have your physician examine you for them so that you do not spend years training for a job that you will not be allowed to hold.

To practice for a test, you must learn what the test is. That means you must know what job you want to apply for and what government you want to work for. You then contact each government and learn what tests are given. Often the government will provide a sample of the test. For a physical agility test or practical test, it should explain exactly what you will have to do. For written tests, governments often issue a booklet; it may only give you an idea of the kinds of questions asked, however. Some commercial publishers sell books with many complete tests in them.

Ask for such books at your library and also contact workers in the occupation and ask them about the tests they took.

If you practice beforehand, you'll be better prepared and less nervous on the day of the test. That will put you ahead of the competition. You can also improve your performance by following this advice:

- Make a list of what you will need at the test center; check it before leaving the house.
- Get a good night's sleep.
- Be at the test center early—at least 15 minutes early.
- Read the instructions carefully; make sure they do not differ from the samples you practiced with.
- Generally, speed counts; do not linger over difficult questions.
- Learn whether guessing is penalized. Most tests are scored by counting up the right answers; guessing is all to the good. Some tests are scored by counting the right answers and deducting partial credit for wrong answers; blind guessing will loose you points—but if you can eliminate two wrong choices in multiple choice tests, a guess might still pay off.

TRIUMPHING AT INTERVIEWS

For many of us, interviews are the most fearsome part of finding a job. But they are also our best chance to show an employer our best side. Interviews are far more flexible than application forms or tests. Use that flexibility to your advantage. As with tests, you can reduce your anxiety and improve your performance by preparing for your interviews ahead of time.

You can begin by considering what interviewers want to know. You represent a risk to the agency. A hiring mistake is expensive in terms of lost productivity, wasted training money, and the cost of finding a replacement. To lessen the risk, interviewers try to select people who are highly motivated, understand what the job entails, and show that they can perform it.

You show that you are highly motivated by learning about the agency before the interview, by dressing appropriately, and by being well mannered—which means that you greet the interviewer by name, you do not chew gum, you do not smoke, you listen attentively, and you thank the interviewer at the end of the session. You also show motivation by expressing interest in the job at the end of the interview.

You show that you understand what the job entails and that you can perform it when you explain how your qualifications prepare you for specific duties as described in the announcement and when you ask intelligent questions about the nature of the work and the training provided new workers.

One of the best ways to prepare for an interview is to have some practice sessions with a friend or two. here is a list of some commonly asked questions to get you started.

- Why did you apply for this job?
- What do you know about this job or agency?
- Why did you choose this career?
- Why should I hire you?
- What would you do if . . . (Usually filled in with a work-related crisis)
- How would you describe yourself?
- What would you like to tell me about yourself?
- What are your major strengths?
- What are your major weaknesses?
- What type of work do you like to do best?

Your strategy should be to concentrate on the job and your ability to do it no matter what the question seems to be asking. If asked for a strength, mention something job-related. If asked for a weakness, mention a job-related strength (you work too hard, you worry too much about details, you always have to see the big picture). If asked about a disability or a specific negative factor in your past—a criminal record, a failure in school, being fired—be prepared to stress what you learned from the experience, how you have overcome the shortcoming, and how you are now in a position to do a better job. Salary negotiation is a special subject in itself. Avoid discussing salaries and fringe benefits until you have a job offer.

So far, only the interviewer's questions have been discussed. But an interview will be a two-way conversation. You really do need to learn more about the position to find out if you want the job. Given how frustrating it is to look for a job, you do not want to take just any position only to learn after two weeks that you can't stand the place and have to look for another job right away. Here are some questions for you to ask the interviewer.

- What would a day on this job be like?
- Whom would I report to? May I meet this person?
- Whom would I supervise? May I meet them?
- How important is this job to the agency?
- What training programs are offered?
- What advancement opportunities are available?
- Why did the last person leave this job?
- What is that person doing now?
- What is the greatest challenge of this position?

After you ask such questions, listen carefully to the interviewer's answer, then, if at all possible, point to something about yourself that fits with the answer. You might notice that questions about salary and fringe benefits are not included in the above list. Your focus at a first interview should be the agency and what you can do for it, not what the agency can pay you. The salary range will be given in the position announcement and information on the usual fringe benefits will be available from the personnel department. Once you have been offered a position, you can negotiate about the salary.

At the end of the interview, be sure you know what the next step will be: whether you should contact the agency again, whether you should provide more information, whether more interviews must be conducted, and when a final decision should be reached. End on a positive note by reaffirming your interest in the position and pointing out why you will be a good choice. Thank the interviewer.

Immediately after the interview, make notes of what went well and what you would like to improve on next time. To show your interest in the position, send a follow-up letter to the interviewer, providing further information on some point raised in the interview and thanking the interviewer once again.

CHAPTER 6

FINDING THE JOB

If you seek a job in a merit system, this chapter is for you. If you want to learn more about elected positions, see the chapter "Running for Office."

WHERE TO START

The federal government, every state, most cities, and many counties have agencies that provide information about how jobs are filled. The names and addresses of many of them are listed in the appendix. You can learn the names of others from government directories, which can be found in the public library. The government section of telephone books also indicates whom to contact for job information, in many cases.

Two other government agencies also try to help job seekers. One is the *Job Service,* which provides employment information and counseling for both government and nongovernment jobs. The other is the *public library.* Besides directories and job announcements, it will have many other books and some magazines that give advice on finding work.

Professional organizations and unions are among the nongovernment groups that often have information for job seekers. No matter which occupations interest you, some association of people who work in it probably exists, and you can find these listed under *Associations* in the yellow pages of the phone book. Your library probably also has a directory of associations. Some associations publish explicit career information, but even those that do not often have useful material such as a periodical that contains articles on salaries and working conditions or help-wanted ads and position announcements. Even the association's membership directory is helpful because it will name people with whom you can discuss the occupation. These materials are often available on request from the association.

FINDING ANNOUNCEMENTS

The sources of information given above are useful for both general leads and specific help. But once you decide on an occupation and a government career, specific information is what you need.

In order to land a government job, you usually have to find an announcement, the different kinds of which are described in the previous chapter. First you need an announcement that a test is being given or that people's qualifications for an occupation are being evaluated. You need to find *position* or *job vacancy announcements* so that you can apply for a job, since no matter how highly you are rated by a personnel department, you usually have to discover your own opening. An evaluation isn't a guarantee; it's a fishing license. And be sure to start looking long before you'll need a job. As was pointed out in the last chapter, landing a job can easily take more than a year.

Governments publicize their announcements several ways. The following are the most common:

- *Bulletin boards* in government buildings are almost always used. The obvious place is near the personnel office, but announcements are also found elsewhere. The state of Connecticut lists 70 places where it posts announcements, including courthouses and hospitals.
- *Public libraries,* perhaps because branches are often located throughout a government's area, often receive copies of all announcements.
- *Local newspapers* print brief notices of job openings in the help-wanted section.

- *Job Banks,* which are run by the Job Service, a state agency, usually list both state and local position announcements as well as other jobs. The locations of Job Service offices are given in the state government section of telephone books. The Job Bank, or listing, is also sometimes available at libraries and schools.
- *Community organizations,* such as the YMCA, NAACP, and churches, receive announcements; Baltimore sends such notices to over 100 organizations.
- *College placement offices* often post job announcements; you can usually check the bulletin board even if you are not enrolled.
- *Newspapers and other periodicals* aimed at government workers—federal, state, or local—carry position announcements. Examples of such newspapers are *The Chief* in New York City and the *Federal Times* in Washington, D.C. Besides the announcements, the articles in such newspapers can point you toward agencies that are likely to begin hiring even before an official announcement is issued.
- *Publications of associations of government workers* carry both job notices and pertinent articles on trends. Titles of such publications appear throughout this book.
- *Publications of associations in fields with many government workers,* such as civil engineering and nursing, also carry both help-wanted ads and informative articles. These publications, too, are listed throughout this book.
- *Commercial publications* also collect and print the job vacancy announcements for several agencies or governments; some such publications are limited to a single level of government, such as federal, state, city, or county; others focus on all governments within a region. Titles of some of these publications are given in the appendix. Check with a librarian to learn which would be most useful to you.
- *Recorded telephone messages.* Many governments, especially the larger ones, have regularly updated recorded messages concerning openings and announcements. The number will usually be listed in the government section of the telephone book under the agency's name.

When you find an announcement, make careful note of the following information:

- The date by which you must apply.
- If the announcement is for an examination, the titles of the occupations covered.
- If the announcement is for positions, the titles of the jobs and where they are located.
- The minimum education and experience required.
- The job duties.
- Where to send your application.
- Whom to contact for more information, if stated.

If you are going to be evaluated on the basis of your education and experience rather than by a test, the announcement's description of the job's duties can help you use the terms the personnel office will recognize when you write about your qualifications.

AND PUTTING MORE IRONS IN THE FIRE

Finding announcements should not be the only focus of your job search, however. Many jobs are filled without such a notice being made; in other cases, the notice is put up only after a preferred job candidate has been found. Therefore, in addition to looking for announcements, you should look for potential employers in other ways.

Begin with relatives and friends who either work for the government or have the kind of occupation you want in the private sector. Government is so large that you or a member of your family is bound to know someone with a government job. Such a person can start you on the track of finding the right people to contact. One contact will lead to another, and you might eventually find someone who is just getting ready to hire a new worker. Even if the contacts don't point you toward a job, they can frequently offer valuable advice on filling out applications and on the current job market.

You should also contact the agencies that you know employ people who do the kind of work you want. You can then write, telephone, or visit the agency.

Private employment agencies listed under employment services in the yellow pages may also have information about government jobs. If you use such an agency, make sure you know if you are going to have to pay any fees, and if so, how much. In most cases, the person who hires you will pay the fee, not you. In others, you will pay the fee. Most agencies are reputable and will give you fair service for your money; but some are not. If you do have to pay, you should grill the agency to learn exactly what it can do for you before you make any final decision or sign any papers. Ask for the names of other clients and contact them to learn if they feel the agency's fees were worth paying; contact their supervisors, too, to learn if they use the agency very often. You can also check with the Better Business Bureau to ask whether or not the private employment agency has a good business history.

Lastly, you can go back to the beginning of this chapter. The sources of general information given there can also point you toward contacts with hiring officials in the government.

CHAPTER 7

RUNNING FOR OFFICE

A great many office holders in state and local government are elected. Exactly which officials are elected varies a great deal, but among them may be the following:

State:
Legislator, delegate, representative, senator, or assemblyman
Governor
Lieutenant governor
Attorney general
Treasurer
Secretary of state
Auditor
Superintendent of education or public instruction
Member of board of education
Commissioner of agriculture
Commissioner of public utilities
Controller
Insurance commissioner
Commissioner of public lands
Commissioner of labor
Commissioner of mines
Judge
Local:
Member of the board of supervisors, city council, town council, or board of commissioners

Mayor
Assessor
Auditor
Clerk—town, county, or court
Coroner
District attorney or county prosecutor
Health officer
Public defender
Public administrator
Recorder
Sheriff
Superintendent of schools
Member of the board of education
Surveyor
Tax Collector
Treasurer
Judge

The decision to seek one of these jobs should not be taken lightly. But these are the jobs where real change is possible.

DECIDING TO RUN

Dick Simpson, a veteran of many campaigns, says that the decision to seek an elected office results from a combination of ambition and altruism. You should also have the ability to win. Like any major choice, the decision to run for office can be broken into smaller components. Here are some questions to consider.

- *Do you have the time to mount a campaign?*
- Will your job suffer?
- Will family responsibilities suffer?
- Do you have the support to mount a campaign?
- Will your family approve?
- Will your family help?
- Will regular party members help?

- Are you known in the community?
- Will civic organizations or their members support you?
- *Do you have the financial resources for the campaign?*
- How much money will be needed? (The winner spent more than $5 million in a gubernatorial campaign in Louisiana, but a candidate in North Dakota spent less than $200,000 to beat an incumbent. Local races are usually far less expensive.)
- What finance laws govern the election? *The Book of States* has this information for state offices.
- Will individuals and groups that support you back that commitment with money?
- *Do you meet the requirements for the job?*
- What are the age and residency requirements?
- Is a particular occupational certification, such as a law degree, required?
- Can you meet the filing dates?
- Must you submit a citizen's petition?
- What is the filing fee?
- *Are you qualified for the job?*
- Is special knowledge needed?
- Do you have positions on the issues?
- *Will the voters recognize that you have the qualifications?*
- Are you known to them?
- Are your positions close enough to theirs so that you can make a case?
- *Can you afford to win?*
- *Do you deserve the job?*
- Are you the best person for the position? Why?
- How will the community benefit from your winning?
- *Do you really want the job?*

Sandy Huseby, in *How To Win an Election,* puts the question, "Can you afford to win?" first on his list of things to ask yourself. Remember that some of these jobs are very time consuming but pay very little. You must ask if you can live on the salary, if you can afford the time away from your regular career, and if you can afford the time away from your family. In other words, will the benefits balance the commitment in time and energy required?

Incidentally, if you plan a career in politics, pay particular attention to the questions on support. You can build support for a future race by being active in community organizations, building a network of potential supporters, and working in campaigns for other people. Agreement seems universal that the best way to prepare for a campaign is to work in someone else's.

BUILDING A STAFF AND RAISING MONEY

To win an election, all you need do is receive more votes than your opponents. Contacting and convincing voters, therefore, is the obvious path to victory. Doing so requires a combination of people and money; one leads to the other, though neither guarantees victory. Supporters give money; money allows you to build the organization to recruit more supporters.

The basic group of supporters is the campaign committee. Typically, it would have at least the following members:

- Campaign manager (In most cases, the more experienced, the better; nonrunning current and former office holders can recommend people.)
- Treasurer (who must be thoroughly familiar with the finance and financial disclosure laws)
- Campaign chairperson (to organize all the other workers)
- Publicity chairperson

Naturally, in a larger campaign, the committee might be larger. Publicity, for example, can be split into special events, advertising, and canvassing.

The campaign staff augments the committee. The nucleus of a staff should suggest itself from the questions on support when you decided to run—family, friends, people you know in community organizations. You will also want to recruit many people you do not yet know, of course. Sources of volunteers include the membership lists of organizations, the young Democrats or young Republicans, people who worked in previous campaigns, college campuses, senior centers, and members of political action committees (all PAC's are registered with the Federal Election Commission). Once a start has been made, the staff itself will be a major source of additional volunteers.

Raising money causes more anxiety for many people than building a staff. For example, when asked, "What do you find most difficult about campaigning?" a recent senatorial candidate replied, "Raising money . . . It's the universal complaint of people in politics." However, some people love to do fundraising. And the millions on millions of dollars raised by candidates each year show that many people will contribute to campaigns.

The sources of financial help are pretty much the same as the sources of volunteers. Again, you begin with family and friends, members of organizations that support you, and the contributors to previous campaigns.

LEARNING FROM OTHERS

Needless to say, far more advice is available on campaigning for office than can be given here. Experienced campaigners can provide useful information on using the media, defining the issues, canvassing techniques, money-raising techniques, polling the electorate, using voter roles, determining the amount of money needed, determining the minimum staff requirements, budgeting the cash flow of the campaign, budgeting volunteer's time, planning the candidate's schedule, and many other subjects.

The following organizations are sources of that information:

Democratic National Committee
430 S. Capitol Street SE
Washington, DC 20003

National Women's Political Caucus
1275 K. Street NW
Suite 750
Washington, DC 20005

Republican National Committee
310 First Street SE
Washington, DC 20003

For information on regulations governing candidates and elections, contact the board of elections, clerk's office, or secretary of state's office. Information on federal regulations is available from the Federal Election Commission, 999 E Street NW, Washington, DC 20463.

Besides the above organizations, many books have been written that are filled with nuts-and-bolts information. A few have a very specific ideological bent; that does not make their advice less useful, however. The following are some of these books:

Beaudry, Ann E., *Running To Win—State Legislative Campaigns*. Washington, DC: 1986. National Abortion Rights.

Guzzetta, S.J., *The Campaign Manual*. Alexandria, VA: Campaign Publishing Co., 1987.

Huseby, Sandy, *How To Win an Election: A Complete Guide to Running a Successful Campaign*. New York, NY: St. Martin's Press, 1983.

Simpson, Dick., *Winning Elections*. Chicago, IL: Swallow Press, 1982.

Yorke, Harvey, and Liz Doherty, *The Candidate's Handbook for Winning Local Elections*. Novato, CA: Harvey Yorke, 1982.

CHAPTER 8

JOBS THROUGHOUT THE GOVERNMENT

Most government occupations are concentrated in one agency or another. Some occupations, however, are found in all sorts of different agencies. The largest of these occupations are discussed in this chapter.

PROFESSIONAL OCCUPATIONS

Among the professional occupations spread through many government agencies are accountant, lawyer, computer programmer and computer systems analyst, office manager, purchasing agent, and personnel officer. These jobs usually require at least a college diploma in a field related to the occupation, although technical and clerical employees are sometimes promoted into a few of them.

ACCOUNTANTS

Governments make no profits and pay no taxes, but government accountants still have plenty to do. Accountants keep track of an organization's assets and liabilities. For a business, that includes figuring out if the year ended with a profit or in the red and completing complicated tax forms. For a government, it includes preparing budgets, keeping track of incoming money (both taxes and transfers from higher governments) and payments, estimating income and expenditures for the next year or more, and analyzing the cost of doing something different ways.

Accountants use calculators and computers to organize the data they work with. They generally work in well-lit, comfortable offices for 40 hours a week.

What you should bring to this occupation. Besides enjoying working with numbers, an accountant must have an interest in detail. In addition, accountants need communication skills to report the results of their analysis in writing and orally.

The majority of accountants have bachelor's degrees in accounting. Many accountants, however, began working as bookkeepers or accounting clerks and were promoted into accounting positions.

The rewards. Accountants find the orderliness of accounting procedures satisfying. If you do not like working with details and do not value order you probably will not enjoy accounting.

The average salary for 1990 was $36,400, according to the Bureau of Labor Statistics. The range of salaries for government accountants in 1990 was from $16,000 to $61,316, according to the International Personnel Management Association. They receive the usual fringe benefits.

Where to find a job. In 1990, 90,000 people worked as accountants for state and local government. Budget agencies, controllers offices, tax assessors' offices, treasury departments, and other agencies that are responsible for financial matters or auditing services have a higher than average proportion of these workers. The employment of accountants throughout the economy is projected to increase faster than the average during the next decade.

Where to learn more. Several associations provide information about accounting, including the following:

American Institute of Certified Public Accountants
1211 Avenue of the Americas
New York, NY 10036.

American Society of Women Accountants
35 East Wacker Drive, Ste. 2250
Chicago, IL 60601

LAWYERS

Lawyers who work for state and local governments draft ordinances and legislation, represent the government in hearings and trials, and teach in public law schools. Most spend much of their time researching legal matters. To practice, lawyers must be members of the state bar, which requires passing the bar exam; in most states, only law school graduates may take the exam. Average salaries for lawyers is in the upper third for all wage earners; the average for all attorneys was $110,000 in 1990. The median annual salary for government attorneys was $41,000 in 1990, according to the International Personnel Management Association, however salaries ranged from $23,800 to $91,000. According to the International City Management Association, the average salary of municipal attorneys in 1988 was $42,000. This is a moderate-size occupation, employing a total of about 250,000 people in 1988. State and local governments employed about 42,000 lawyers in 1988. Most lawyers work for firms in the legal services industry. Many other people with law degrees make use of their training in business or government, but do not practice. To learn more about this occupation you can also contact unions or associations such as the American Bar Association, 750 N. Lake Shore Drive, Chicago, IL 60611.

A rapidly growing area of employment is that of the legal assistant—commonly called *paralegal*. As costs increase, the employment of paralegals will increase. To learn more about this profession write to:

American Association for Paralegal Education
P.O. Box 40244
Overland Park, KS 66204

National Association of Legal Assistants, Inc.
1601 South Main Street, Ste. 300
Tulsa, OK 74119

National Paralegal Association
P.O. Box 406
Solebury, PA 18963

See also: Chapter 11.

CLERICAL OCCUPATIONS

The largest occupations found throughout the government are in the clerical group. Secretaries, typists, and word processors alone number almost a million. Other large or important clerical occupations are accounting clerk and bookkeeper, clerical supervisor, file clerk, and town/county clerk. Besides being large, the first three of these occupations have high turnover. This combination means that openings are numerous.

High school graduation is usually the minimum qualification; you can find a job much more easily if you can type at least 40 words per minute. Bookkeeper and accounting clerk jobs may require high school or even junior college courses in business math, bookkeeping, and accounting principals.

WORD PROCESSORS, SECRETARIES, TYPISTS

In some other world, offices might be able to do without secretaries, typists, and word processors, but not in this one. Typists primarily type material either from manuscripts or recorded dictation. Secretaries have many additional duties, including running and maintaining the photocopy machine, organizing files, providing information to callers and visitors, scheduling appointments, and making travel arrangements. Word processors use the latest office equipment to process information and data and to keep records. They are also responsible for editing and storing and revising these materials. Word processors also may be required to function as typists, answer telephones, and operate other office machines. They also need to have good spelling, grammar, and punctuation skills.

Word processing positions are frequently entry-level jobs in the workplace, but they can lead to higher paying jobs later on. They may become supervisors of their department, secretaries, statistical clerks, or stenographers.

Most secretaries, typists, and word processors work in comfortable, well-lit—but sometimes noisy and hectic—offices for 40 hours a week.

What you should bring to this occupation. Successful secretaries are able to handle many things at once, organize their own work, and get along with others. Increasingly, they must be adaptable because of the rapid introduction of new word processing equipment. Each new machine means a change in how to do things, and new machines seem to come along just when the last one has been mastered.

Secretaries and typists, too, should be good spellers and know the essentials of English punctuation and grammar. They also need some mechanical skills to maintain and perform minor repairs to the equipment they use.

Few employers hire typists who cannot type at least 40 words per minute. Higher speeds are preferred. A high school education is usually required.

The rewards. These workers receive satisfaction from contributing to the success of their organizations; the more they value those goals, the more satisfied they are with their work—a point worth considering when you apply for a job.

Typists and secretaries are also able to advance to supervisory positions; some become administrative assistants or office managers. The chances for advancement depend in part on the way an organization is set up, and you may require additional education. Among the sources of dissatisfaction for these workers are low salaries and lack of prestige within the organization.

The average salary for typists in 1990 was $18,000; secretaries earned $21,700. These figures indicate that average salary for typists is in the lower third for all wage earners; and the average for secretaries is in the middle third for all wage earners; government salaries are comparable. Salaries vary widely, however, depending on the skills and responsibilities of the worker. Secretaries and typists receive the usual fringe benefits.

Where to learn more. General information about this occupation is available from the following association:

Professional Secretaries International
  1502 NW Ambassador Drive
  P.O. Box 20404
  Kansas City, MO 64195-0404

A note on stenographers: Extensive use of recorded dictation has resulted in a decline in the employment of stenographers throughout the economy, but the decline has not been as great in state and local government. In fact, while state and local governments employ 20 percent of all secretaries and 31 percent of all typists, the 115,000 stenographers they employ represent 43 percent of the people in the occupation. Many of these stenographers are court reporters who operate stenotype machines, which requires special training. More information about court reporters appears in the chapter on the court system.

OTHER CLERICAL OCCUPATIONS

Bookkeepers and accounting clerks keep track of the money that an organization takes in and pays out. They keep records in journals and ledgers or on computer disks. High school graduates usually qualify for these jobs, especially if they have learned business arithmetic, bookkeeping, and principals of accounting. The average salary for accounting clerks is in the middle third for all wage earners; the median salary in 1990 was $17,000.

File clerk is an entry-level job in many large agencies. The clerk sorts letters, bills, contracts, or other documents according to the alphabet, a numerical code, or some other system and puts them where they belong. The clerk also finds and retrieves an item when it is needed. Some clerks classify the material to begin with. A high school education is usually required. The average annual salary was $13,000 in 1990.

Town or county clerks act as secretaries to the governing board, recording the minutes of meetings, answering letters, and preparing reports. They also issue and keep records of official documents, such as marriage licenses, birth certificates, and land deeds. This is usually an elected office. The average salary in 1988 was $27,000 according to the International City Management Association. For more information, speak to the clerk in your area.

CLERICAL OCCUPATIONS—THE FUTURE

As the Information Age continues to develop and emerging technologies become commonplace in all offices, including state and local governments, job titles and descriptions will change also. More and more secretaries are now known as *administrative assistants.* The duties of the job have grown and widened until the new title more accurately reflects what anyone holding the position does in a typical day.

As new technology replaces such long-used office machines as dictaphones there will be fewer (except as we noted before—in courts) opportunities in the field. And just as there will be fewer and fewer typists, there will be a rapidly growing need for trained *word processors.* Check the ads in your local paper, and you will see how many require knowledge of the various systems now in place in even the smallest office. In larger offices there usually appears a department devoted exclusively to word processing—much like the now almost obsolete "typing pool."

This is an area of employment in which anyone who will make the effort to acquire new skills as new technology comes into the workplace will advance. Anyone trained to operate tomorrow's office machines will be a prime candidate for supervisory positions.

CRAFT AND BLUE-COLLAR OCCUPATIONS

Several technical, service, operative, craft, and repairer occupations also have large numbers of workers in many different government agencies. These occupations include building custodian, electrician, engineering and science technician, general maintenance repairer, and guard. Some of these jobs are very routine; others are extremely varied. Some require no particular education or experience; qualifying for others takes years of training. Salaries naturally reflect these differences.

Automobile mechanics find out what is wrong with a car and fix it; they must be able to use tools and read shop manuals; some specialize in certain types of repairs, such as transmissions or tune-ups, but most do a little bit of everything. Average wages are within the middle 40 percent for all wage earners; the average wage in 1990 was $25,800. Employment in state and local governments was about 50,000 that year. Major employers in state and local government would be departments that own many vehicles, such as police and fire departments. The occupation is projected to grow faster than average through 1995; turnover will make even more jobs available. Further information is available in *Opportunities in Automotive Services* by Robert Weber (Lincolnwood, IL: National Textbook Co., 1989), and from these two associations: Automotive Service Industry Association, 444 North Michigan Avenue, Chicago, IL 60611; Automotive Service Association, 1901 Airport Freeway, Ste. 100, P.O. Box 929, Bedford, TX 76095-0929. *Automotive News* and *Motor Service Magazine* are among the many periodicals that carry articles related to this occupation.

Electricians are skilled craft workers with years of training. They install and repair the wiring in government buildings. Apprenticeship programs provide training. Electricians must be licensed. Average salaries for electricians are in the middle third for all wage earners; average weekly earnings in 1990 were $625. This is a moderate-size occupation, with a total employment of 542,000 in 1990; state and local governments employed more than 30,000 electricians that year. Large school systems and hospitals also employ many thousands of electricians. You can contact unions or associations such as the following: International Brotherhood of Electrical Workers, 1125 15th Street NW, Washington, DC 20005.

Engineering and science technicians test equipment and use laboratory or engineering instruments. This title refers to a large group of occupations that call for similar levels of skill and training, although the specific duties vary widely. Among these occupations are drafter, electrical and electronics technician, civil engineering technician, surveyor, biological technician, sanitation technician, and pump technician. Drafting, surveying, technical, and laboratory experience or courses in technical schools or community colleges are helpful in qualifying for these jobs, but some openings are available for high school graduates. Salaries depend in part on the specific occupation. The average salary for drafters was $27,200 in 1990. The average salary for electrical and electronics technicians was $24,000 in 1990. The average annual salary for engineering technicians in 1990 was $29,800. Starting salaries for those with no more than a high school diploma are about the same as in entry-level clerical jobs. Total employment in these occupations exceeded 1,200,000 in the economy as a whole in 1988; state and local governments employed about 100,000 of these workers. A pamphlet, "Drafting as a Career," is available from the American Design and Drafting Association, 5522 Norbeck Road, Ste. 391, Rockville, MD 20853. A series of pamphlets on engineering technician occupations is published by the American Association of Engineering Societies, 19th Street NW, Ste. 608, Washington, DC 20036.

General maintenance repairers combine the skills of a carpenter, electrician, mechanic, painter, plumber, and plasterer, performing general maintenance and making minor repairs as needed. They work with a great variety of hand and power tools. A high school diploma may be required, but more important is the ability to do the work. The salary range is wide, going from little above the minimum wage almost to the upper third for all wage earners; in 1988, salaries ranged from $6 to $13 an hour, depending on the skill required for particular positions. State and local governments employ about 160,000 of these workers, mostly in schools and hospitals. Average growth is projected between now and 1995. Growth combined with turnover should result in thousands of jobs becoming available each year. To learn more about this occupation, visit the Job Service, listed in the state government section of your phone book.

Guards patrol buildings when they are closed and keep watch over their entrances when they are open. A high school diploma is usually preferred, but not always required. In 1988, the average hourly wage was $6.08. There are about 62,000 guards employed in state and local government. Schools, hospitals, and government office buildings frequently employ guards. There are currently over 1,200,000 people employed as guards and security officers. The field is expected to grow at more than the average rate at least until the year 2000.

CHAPTER 9

ADMINISTRATION AND LEGISLATION

General control jobs refer to *legislative, governmentwide adminis-trative,* and *judiciary functions.* Law making is the one function shared by every government. The laws are passed by city councils, county boards, or state legislatures and enforced by city managers, mayors, or governors. Judges and justices of the peace determine if laws have been broken and by whom. All these occupations make up a very mixed bag. Many of those in them were either elected by the citizens or appointed by someone who was elected. They are what politics is all about.

State legislature, city councils, and county boards perform the same functions for their governments that Congress does for the federal government. They determine what the government should do and how services should be paid for. They hold hearings to consider new laws or ordinances, approve the government's budget, and either appoint or confirm the appointments of policy-making officials. Employees of the legislative branch include clerical workers, specialists such as legal analysts who can act as advisors, and lawyers. Total legislative employment is far smaller than executive employment, however, accounting for less than 4 percent of total state and local government employment; for example, in California, the state legislature employs only about two thousand people.

Financial administration keeps track of the government's revenues and expenditures. Collecting taxes, preparing budgets, and monitoring expenditures are jobs done by every government. Appraising real estate is a common job at the local level.

The Census Bureau groups most of these workers in two categories: *general control* and *financial administration*. Total state and local government employment in these categories was about 760,000 in 1988. The proportion of these workers is higher locally than at the state level. The country's cities have more than 12,000 mayors, 6,000 clerks, 5,000 financial directors, 3,000 planning directors, 12,000 police and fire chiefs, and 5,000 directors of public works, according to the International City Management Association.

CITY MANAGERS

Who runs the store when a committee is in charge? That's the question confronting cities and towns with a council-manager form of government. And the answer is the same for both store and city: a professional manager. Cities and towns have many different departments, each of which takes care of particular functions, such as police protection or street repair. City managers see that all the departments run smoothly.

Depending on the laws of the state and the will of the council, city managers may appoint the department heads. They usually prepare the city budget and submit it for approval. They may also suggest changes in city ordinances or policies.

City managers officially work a 40-hour week, but most will put in many more hours than that. Much of their time is spent in an office, but they may also have to travel throughout the city, attend council meetings, and so on.

What you should bring to this occupation?

City managers usually have a master's degree in public administration, which would include such courses as municipal law, finance, and political aspects of urban problems. An internship of 6 to 12 months may be required. They frequently start their careers as assistants before becoming managers.

Managers are usually appointed by a council or mayor; their contracts are subject to renewal on a regular basis.

The rewards. Successful city managers have the satisfaction of performing a very complex job well. They also have the problem of pleasing several different politicians. One drawback is that advancement may require moving to new cities several times in a career.

In 1990, the salary range was from $42,559 to $109,000, according to the International City Manager Association. City and county managers receive standard fringe benefits—such as vacation and sick leave—and many receive additional benefits, such as an automobile, moving expenses, and liability insurance.

Where to find a job. This is a small occupation, although at least 5,000 worked as appointed managers in cities and counties in 1988, and perhaps three times as many worked as management assistants. The major employers are cities ranging from 10,000 to 500,000 in population.

Information about this occupation is available from the following organizations:

International City Management Association
777 N. Capitol Street NE, Ste. 500
Washington, DC 20002-4201

National Civic League
1445 Market Street
Denver, CO 80202

LEGISLATORS/COUNCIL MEMBERS

Making laws could be called the first function of government, for it is only after a society has agreed on the rules which govern it that the executive can enforce them and the judiciary can determine infractions of them. In fact, we had a legislature, the Continental Congress, even before we had a country.

The duties of city, county, or state legislator do not differ *in kind* from those of the most powerful senator in Washington. One might consider a multithousand dollar project to build a turn-lane at a busy intersection, while the other is concerned with the multibillion dollar interstate highway system, but both must strike a balance between the desirability of a government provided service and the ability of the taxpayers to pay for it.

Relatively few of these jobs are full-time, year-round positions. State legislatures usually meet just part of the year; some meet only every other year. Governing boards of cities and counties are more likely to hold sessions throughout the year, meeting one day or evening every week or two, but—at least in theory—the board or council members work fewer than 40 hours a week.

What you should bring to this occupation. Concern for the public welfare is probably the chief characteristic of these officials. Legislators and council members should be able to analyze complex issues and propose solutions. They must understand how their government operates, and they must be able to persuade others—both voters and other members of the body—to accept their ideas.

These are elected positions; the voters determine what experience, education, and ability are required. Most state legislators are management or professional workers; about 30 percent were lawyers in 1990. Relatively few are clerical or blue-collar workers. Representatives from agriculture are relatively common in some areas, however, considering how few farmers there are in the economy as a whole.

The rewards. Successful legislators have the satisfaction of seeing their vision of society become reality, at least in part. They also experience the frustration of not being able to put all their plans into action.

Salaries and other benefits vary enormously, ranging from little more than the minimum wage to more than $30,000 a year, depending on the size of the government. Annual salaries for state legislators in 1989 ranged from $100 to $48,000.

Where to learn more. Attending public sessions of the governing board is one way to learn about these occupations. Working in a campaign is one of the best ways to learn what an election is like. The local government itself, the board of elections (or some similar body), and local political parties can provide information on the requirements for specific positions.

ASSESSORS

Assessors evaluate taxable property. While the federal government raises most of its money from income taxes, a large proportion of state and local taxes is based on real estate or other property. Assessors determine the value of the property. They are usually elected or appointed by elected officials. Deputy assessors, or appraisers, however, are more likely to be merit system employees. They often have an associate's or bachelor's degree with a major in real estate or assessing. The salary range is as great as the range in size of local governments, reaching from $15,000 to $60,000 a year. In small towns, assessing may be a part-time job or even one of the duties of the town clerk.

CHAPTER 10

COURT SYSTEM

Following the model of the United States Constitution, state and local governments have three branches: *legislative* and *executive*—which are sometimes combined at the local level—and *judicial.* Among the names used for parts of the judicial branch are supreme court, court of appeals, superior court, circuit court, and district court. Judges run the third branch—which administers the court system—and preside over trials, hearings, and grand jury proceedings. Other occupations in the judicial branch include bailiff or marshall, magistrate, court reporter, public defender, and court clerk. Typically, the judicial is the smallest branch of government in terms of employment and expenditures.

JUDGES

Judges administer justice in our system of government. They control proceedings in the courtroom. In jury trials, they also interpret the law for the jury, explaining the possible verdicts, for example. In addition to presiding at trials, judges are also administrators. They are ultimately responsible for the smooth functioning of the judicial branch of government.

Judges usually work a standard 40-hour week in comfortable surroundings.

What you should bring to this occupation. Judges must be able to think clearly and analyze complex problems. They must also be able to win elections or impress those who do, since judges are either elected by the people or chosen by elected officials. They should possess extensive knowledge of law; and most all have law degrees, although a degree requirement is not quite universal.

The rewards. Successful judges have the satisfaction of performing a difficult job well and contributing to the protection of society. They also have the problem of facing innumerable difficult decisions; both the wrongly condemned innocent person and the mistakenly freed criminal who attacks another victim weigh heavily on a conscientious judge's mind.

Salaries for state judges averaged $69,400 in 1989, according to the Council of State Governments. Most judges enjoy better than average fringe benefits. Elected judges, however, have less job security than most government workers.

Where to learn more. You can best learn about this occupation by talking with a judge. Since a law degree is required, sources of information given in Chapter 11 are also relevant.

COURT REPORTERS

Court reporters are specialized stenographers who, using stenotype machines or shorthand, make word-for-word records of court proceedings, hearings, and legislative sessions. They may also be called shorthand reporters, hearing reporters, or legal reporters. A recording speed as high as 225 words per minute may be required, although 160 is sufficient for some jobs. Besides recording dictation, court reporters may also type, transcribe their notes, or dictate their notes for a typist; increasingly, however, the notes can be transcribed by computer. Shorthand reporters can learn their skills in two-year programs at post-high school technical institutes and junior colleges. Salaries are better than those of other clerical workers. This is a relatively small occupation for the clerical field, but demand is often greater than the supply. To learn more about this occupation, you can contact the National Shorthand Reporters Association, 118 Park Street SE, Vienna, VA 22180. A publication which may be useful to you is the *National Shorthand Reporter*.

CHAPTER 11

LAWYERS AND PARALEGALS

LAWYERS

Attorneys are employed in substantial numbers in state and local governments. They are an integral part of the criminal justice system and may work for a state attorney general or in county courts as prosecutors or public defenders. Often, the jobs in these offices are filled by recent law school graduates who need to gain some experience, or need immediate employment to begin paying back educational loans. Many recent graduates do not have the funds to open a private practice, and if they can't get quick placement in a law firm, they turn to these jobs to get started. It is also an excellent training ground for young lawyers who envision a career in elective office. The workings of a state's attorney's office are often high-profile and will make those who work there familiar names and faces to the public.

In addition, the almost twenty thousand municipalities in the United States employ large numbers of lawyers who help develop local statutes, interpret federal and state regulations, establish enforcement procedures, and argue cases on behalf of the city. Smaller communities may retain lawyers who also have a practice that allows them time to work on contract. Special districts, school districts, and townships will also either have their own lawyers or contract on a per hour basis.

Still other lawyers may work for nonprofit organizations, trade associations, contracting and consulting firms, and lobbying groups. While none of these categories is actually employed by governments, they often work with legislatures developing laws, conducting research, and contracting for other services.

What you should bring to this occupation. First, of course, you must have completed your degree at an accredited law school and then have passed the bar examination. After completing the first phase you must then bring your skills in managing people, communicating both orally and in written papers, and some specialized technical knowledge to your work. Computers have moved into the world of law in a grand style. Lawyers now own software that substitutes to some degree for the long hours in law libraries. They will then use a computer to organize and index the material their software has led them to. Tax lawyers make wide use of computers to make computations and to explore various tax strategies. Finally, lawyers must be capable of an extreme degree of discretion in terms of keeping clients' legal affairs in the strictest of confidence. Trading war stories about interesting, but confidential, cases is not an option that a good lawyer has.

The rewards. Lawyers are well-paid professionals whose working conditions, incomes, and opportunities for variety in their work are exceptionally high. There is no problem of their work being seasonal, and, curiously enough, the harder times get—the more lawyers are needed to deal with such events as bankruptcies, divorces, and foreclosures. While law practices are not totally recession-proof, they are often the last to feel economic stress.

Where to learn more. Annually, the American Bar Association publishes *A Review of Legal Education in the United States,* which provides information on all of the law schools approved by the American Bar Association. You can get one copy free from them by writing to:

Information Services
  American Bar Association
  750 N. Lake Shore Drive
  Chicago, IL 60611

Starting salaries in state and local governments average about $26,000 per year. However, the experience that young lawyers gain will propel them into positions of greater responsibility and greater financial rewards in a short time. Whether they go on to private practice, elective office, or judgeships, they will be among the top occupations in annual income within a decade after leaving law school.

PARALEGALS

Lawyers are increasingly working with paralegals—sometimes called "legal assistants." There is much work to be done in law offices that does not require a law school graduate. In general, paralegals will do research and background work for lawyers. As costs increase, more and more legal departments in state and local government have only a few lawyers and dozens of paralegals in their employ.

In government, paralegals will analyze legal materials for use within the office, maintain reference files, conduct research, collect and analyze evidence for hearings, and prepare informational material for their own office use and for the public.

What you should bring to this occupation. Some lawyers will prefer to train their own assistants, or to promote the most capable legal secretaries in the office. Some will search for employees who have completed formal educational programs for the occupation. There are more than 600 of these institutions connected with colleges, universities, community colleges, and proprietary schools. Paralegals need not be certified, but the National Association of Legal Assistants has established standards for voluntary certification.

Paralegals must be skilled in dealing with clients, follow the same ethical guidelines as lawyers in terms of confidentially, have excellent speaking and writing skills, and an ability to work conscientiously, although unsupervised.

The rewards. Paralegals enjoy interesting work, done in pleasant surroundings, better than average salaries for office workers, and the respect of family and friends. Salaries range from $20,000 to $30,000 per year—the median is $24,900. There is, however, little opportunity to rise to a higher position. Paralegals cannot just start practicing law—unless, of course, they learn to like the work enough to enroll in law school. *See also:* Chapter 8.

CHAPTER 12

CORRECTION

Correction departments run prisons and jails and supervise parolees. They employ administrators and food service, health, and maintenance workers, although many of these duties are performed by inmates. The largest group of employees is made up of the correction officers or prison guards, Correction employment by state governments was more than 200,000 in 1988; counties and cities employed 115,000 workers in this category.

CORRECTION OFFICERS

Clanging doors and lonely watch towers mark the working atmosphere of correction officers, who guard prisoners in state penitentiaries and local jails. Their jobs entail keeping careful watch over the prisoners at all times, whether from towers and guard rooms or while escorting them from place to place. They also inspect the prison, checking for signs of damage to locks, doors, and windows and for unsafe or unhealthy conditions. Correction officers also supplement the efforts of psychologists and social workers.

Correction officers usually work an eight-hour day, five days a week, but their shifts may include holidays, weekends, and nights. The working conditions largely depend on the prison environment.

What you should bring to this occupation. Correction officers must have good judgement; they must be able to think and act quickly and effectively.

The usual educational requirement is a high school diploma. Applicants must usually be at least 18, and take a series of tests including a written examination and a test of physical agility. A medical examination may also be required.

Once hired, new officers receive one to six months of training.

The rewards. Correction officers have the satisfaction of protecting society; however, the job can be both stressful and hazardous. They can advance through promotion to sergeant or transfer to a related occupation such as a probation or parole officer, although such a change may require additional education.

The median salary for correction officers employed by states in 1988 was $21,000. They receive standard fringe benefits. Housing is sometimes provided.

Where to find a job. Roughly 315,000 correction officers work for state and local governments. About half work at state penitentiaries and the rest at local jails. Turnover averages 24 percent, which is much higher than for most occupations.

Where to learn more. The following organizations can provide further information:

CONTACT, Inc.
P.O. Box 81826
Lincoln, NB 68501

The American Correctional Association
8025 Laurel Lakes Court
Laurel, MD 20707

OTHER CORRECTION OCCUPATIONS

Parole officers work with the correction or parole department. Parolees are criminals who have been released from prison before completing their sentences. Early release provides an incentive for good behavior and enables the department to see if people can adjust to society while it still has some control over them. Parole officers keep track of the parolees, make certain that parole rules are obeyed, and help them make this adjustment by assisting them in their search for job training and employment or in other ways. Parole officers usually have a bachelor's degree in sociology, psychology, criminology, or correction, and experience in the correction department. Their salaries are comparable to those of social workers; the average salary for social workers is in the lower third for all wage earners.

Probation officers work within the court system, although they are employees of the state correction agency. Before a trial, they investigate the accused person's family background and position in the community in order to recommend whether or not a judge should grant bail. Before a person is sentenced, the officer conducts a similar investigation to see if probation rather than prison should be imposed. After sentencing, officers supervise people on probation to ensure that they obey the rules of their sentences. Probation officers usually have a bachelor's degree in sociology, psychology, criminology, or correction, and experience in the department they work for. As of January 1, 1989, the average entry-level salary for probation officers was $19,000, according to the Criminal Justice Institute.

CHAPTER 13

COMPUTERS

State and local governmental units have lagged behind private employers in their use of computers and computer systems mainly because they have had to await legislative approval to spend the monies to get "on line." As we close out the century, however, most governmental units—even the smallest and most rural—have now come into the computer age. We are currently in the process of reducing the number of clerical positions in government because of the increased productivity the new technology provides. At the same time, from data entry operator to systems programmer, the opportunities for computer-related jobs are many because of the sheer size of the occupation.

PROGRAMMERS—SYSTEMS ANALYSTS—OPERATORS

Programmers are those people who write detailed descriptions of the steps a computer must follow to solve a problem. After designing the program, the programmer will run sample data through the system to determine if it works correctly or if it needs some adjustments. Programmers then prepare instructions for the *operator* who will run the program. Programmers may work alone on a project, or, in the case of large projects, may be part of a team.

Computer programmers usually work from descriptions of a problem presented to them by a *systems analyst*. In some instances, the jobs may be combined and the job will be titled *programmer-analyst*. Others who work in the field are: *data entry clerks, data base managers,* and *computer service technicians.* Most technicians are employed by the manufacturers of the equipment, but some employers, where there is a large enough installation to warrant it, hire their own.

What you should bring to this occupation. There are no standard training requirements for computer-related jobs. Depending on the work to be done and the salary you expect to earn, you can come minimally prepared, or you can come with advanced degrees in computer science, mathematics, or engineering.

Computer programming, system analysis, and other courses can be found in high schools, community colleges, vocational and technical schools, colleges, and universities. There are also home-study courses available. Be prepared to take courses throughout your career. This is an area in which the technology changes very quickly. Courses are offered by employers, by software vendors, and by computer manufacturers. If you expect to advance in your job, get used to the idea of being a periodic student.

The rewards. There are well-paying jobs in all parts of the country. In fact, there are opportunities for experienced people internationally. A job in state or local government could mean preparation for a fascinating job in the private sector. The work is pretty universally done in clean, well-lighted, pleasant surroundings. The opportunities for further training and advancement are many. Most people in the field will work standard workweeks, but occasionally will have to work on weekends when the equipment is not needed for scheduled work.

Where to find a job. Your Job Service office will have openings listed, as will your local or state offices. Watch newspapers for announcements of openings. Search as you would for any other possibility. Additional sources of information are listed here.

American Federation of Information Processing Societies
1899 Preston White Drive
Reston, VA 22091

Association for Computing Machinery
11 West 42nd Street-Third Floor
New York, NY 10036

Data Processing Management Association
505 Busse Highway
Park Ridge, IL 60068

Table 3:

JOB OUTLOOK—COMPUTER-RELATED FIELDS—1988–2000 By Percentage and by Number			
Occupation	*1988*	*Year Estimated 2000 %*	*Year Number change 2000*
Computer Systems Analyst[1]	402,000	54	+214,000
Equipment Operator[2]	316,000	29	+92,000
Word Processors Data Entry Keyer[3]	1,416,000	–6	–82,000
Programmer[4]	51,000	48	+250,000

[1] Will grow faster than the average. Job prospects best for college graduates who combine programming and systems analysis.
[2] Will increase faster than average.
[3] Will decline, but occupation is large.
[4] Expected to grow much faster than average. Job prospects best for college graduates who majored in computer science. Experience in accounting, management, engineering will help.

The ability to think logically, to be patient, and to enjoy the challenge of being unusually accurate will be necessary if you are to find success in the computer world. If those attributes are yours, your horizons are wide open—particularly if you are ambitious and flexible enough to enjoy change. The salary level is also up to you. You may enter at a salary as low as $16,000, but continuing study will take you into the higher reaches of salaried employment.

CHAPTER 14

EDUCATION

In this country, public education is primarily the responsibility of state and local governments. It is also by far the major source of state and local government employment, accounting for almost half of all jobs. Except in Hawaii—which has a state-run school system—elementary schools and high schools are run by local governments; school districts in most states; and county governments in five: Alaska, Maryland, North Carolina, Tennessee, and Virginia. Community colleges and public universities are usually under the control of the state, though they may be largely self-governing. In addition to the schools themselves, each state also has a department of education that sets standards, such as the minimum qualifications for teachers; establishes the curriculum or subjects to be taught; and the school calendar. The local school district, community college, or university hires the teachers, puts up new schools and buildings, closes old ones, and prepares the budget.

Education has the lion's share—the whale's share would be more accurate—of government workers. It employs administrators (such as principals), service and maintenance workers, clerical workers, and, of course, teachers. Employment totals about 7,000,000. People with the following job titles number 50,000 or more (much more in most cases): adult education teacher, building custodian, college and university teacher, counselor, general clerk, institutional cook, kindergarten and elementary school teacher, kitchen helper, librarian, library assistant, maintenance repairer, principal, school bus driver, secondary school teacher, secretary, teacher aide, typist, and vocational education teacher. Many of these occupations are discussed below; some are treated in other chapters, including bus driver, librarian, maintenance repairer, and typist.

The day we met our first teacher, we little suspected how many administrators were needed to bring us together. There are generally three administrative layers in each state's school system.

At the top, usually, is the *state board,* which sets policies, including the curriculum; whether the policies are fairly general or highly specific varies a good deal. In some cases, the state even picks the textbooks. The chief administrator at the state level may be known as the commissioner of education, commissioner of public instruction, or by some other title. This person is elected in 17 states and appointed by elected officials in the other 33.

The middle administrative layer is the *school district,* which may have as many as 800 schools. It, too, usually has a governing board to make final decisions, such as deciding on the budget or determining if the number of teachers and schools is too high or too low. The board is either elected or appointed by elected officials. The day-to-day running of the district is left to the *superintendent.* Besides seeing that the board's decisions are carried out, the superintendent also continually reassesses the needs of the district in order to report them to the board. In larger districts, the superintendent may have several assistants, each of whom is responsible for a group of high schools, middle schools, and elementary schools, or for certain functions throughout the district, such as construction and renovation or teacher evaluation.

The basic administrative unit is the individual school which is managed by a principal.

SCHOOL PRINCIPALS

The principal runs the school in accordance with the rules and policies established by the school board and the superintendent. Principals assign teachers, set schedules, and coordinate school activities. They supervise the maintenance and cafeteria staffs and, of course, the teachers. In a single day, a principal might meet with a teacher concerning an unruly student, go over needed repairs with the custodian, visit a classroom to observe a teacher in action, conduct an assembly, work on next year's budget, counsel a student, and confer with a group of parents about plans for a computer literacy program.

What you should bring to this occupation. Principal is short for 'principal teacher,' and the chief characteristics of successful principals are the same as those of a good teacher: they love children and they love to watch them grow in knowledge and confidence. Principals also need the attributes of any good manager: organization and leadership skills, self-confidence, and decisiveness.

Public school principals must be certified by the state. Almost all have teaching experience and graduate school training, such as a master's degree in school administration, which includes such courses as school management, school law, school finance and budgeting, personnel administration, and community relations.

The rewards. Administration does not offer the immediate satisfactions of teaching. However, principals gain satisfaction from performing a complicated job well and contributing to the education of students. On the other hand, they are subject to criticism from all sides and face innumerable difficult choices in the allocation of the school's resources.

The following, according to the Educational Research Service, were the average salaries in 1988–89: Elementary school: $43,900; junior high school: $46,000; senior high school: $54,000. Principals receive standard fringe benefits of state and local government workers, although they do not receive the longer vacations of teachers.

Where to learn more. These organizations can supply more information about school principals:

Your state's department of education

American Association of School Administrators
1801 North Moore Street
Arlington, VA 22209

The National Association of Secondary School Principals
1904 Association Drive
Reston, VA 22091

ELEMENTARY AND SECONDARY SCHOOL TEACHERS

"If you can read this, thank a teacher." Perhaps you have seen that bumper sticker. The same message could be printed across the cover of every book, newspaper, magazine, and pamphlet that has ever taught you something or made you laugh.

We are all familiar with what teachers do in the classroom: they present new information, conduct exercises and tests, and maintain order. Much of their work takes place outside the classroom, however, preparing lessons, grading papers, increasing their knowledge, and attending meetings.

In the classroom, teachers have different duties depending on their specialty. Broadly speaking, elementary school teachers are responsible for all academic subjects while secondary school teachers usually instruct students in a single subject. Even at the lowest grades, however, some division of labor takes place. For example, physical education is almost always conducted by a teacher trained for that subject. English as a second language, special education, music, and art are other specialties within elementary education. As for high school, a secondary school specialist looks like a generalist to a college professor. Social studies teachers in high school, for example, may be called on to teach history, geography, economics, or sociology, all of which are distinct major fields in college. And a college professor who teaches only medieval English literature would be hard pressed to handle the combination of grammar, literature, and composition that a high school teacher must contend with.

Teachers work when schools are open, which is for about 7 hours at least 180 days a year in most states. They also work when schools are closed, as indicated above. The average workweek was 46 hours in 1988, which is longer than the average for most workers. Working conditions in schools vary widely with regard to heating, air conditioning, lighting, and toilet facilities. More important to most teachers is the variation in class size, resulting from the failure of communities to provide enough teachers and classrooms to have children in class-size groups.

What you should bring to this occupation. Successful teachers love children. They are also creative, intellectually curious, and patient. It goes without saying that they need extraordinary communicating skills with both individuals and groups.

Public school teachers must be certified. The basic educational requirement is a bachelor's degree in education. College graduates who did not take education courses can sometimes meet the requirements through graduate school study.

Besides education, requirements might include citizenship, good health, and good character. Recently, some states have begun to require that new teachers pass competence tests. About half the states require that teachers earn a master's degree within a certain number of years after being hired (so much for the only vacation).

The rewards. The light shining from the face of a child who has just grasped a new idea is, perhaps, the greatest satisfaction of teaching. Teachers in most school systems also enjoy a good deal of independence. Drawbacks of the profession include relatively low salaries for the amount of education required, a loss of prestige in the last generation, and extensive paper-work that can lessen contact time with students. Some teachers also complain about the difficulty of maintaining order and discipline in the classroom.

Teachers can advance by becoming administrators or specialists such as counselors. Both moves require further education. In fact, most teachers remain in teaching.

The average salary for public elementary school teachers in 1989 was $28,900; secondary school teachers received $30,300, on average. They receive the usual fringe benefits and more vacation time than most workers. They do not get quite as much time off as they seem to, however, because of their need to continue their own education and improve their skills.

Where to find a job. Public elementary and secondary schools employed more than 2,400,000 classroom teachers in 1989.

The job outlook for teachers is currently going through a transition. Until the mid-1980s, for a dozen years or so, we had a surplus of teachers in certain areas. The number of school-age children was falling, but the number of people being trained to teach was not. The result was a surplus of new teachers for most fields, although in some fields, including industrial arts and physical education for girls, there were shortages.

More recently, enrollment in education schools has declined, and the number of young, school-age children has risen. In 1981, 70 percent of the Class of 1980's education majors were working as elementary and secondary school teachers. This compares well with other fields that are thought to have good records in job placement, such as engineering and accounting.

The number of teachers needed between now and 1995 largely depends on the number of children in various age groups. Projections indicate that the number of elementary school students will continue to rise; the secondary school population will decline somewhat for a few years and then rise again to about its current level; the college age population will decrease dramatically in the 1990s.

Your chances of finding a job depend not only on demand, however, but also on the supply of people able to do the work. Projections of the future supply of teachers are much less certain than demand projections, since the supply depends on the free choice of millions of people. Complicating the picture is the very large number of qualified teachers who are not now employed. Still, given (1) the current level of enrollments in education schools, (2) the fast growth projected at the elementary level, (3) the annual replacement rate for employed teachers who leave the occupation, and (4) the huge size of the occupation, qualified graduates of accredited education programs should be able to find employment in elementary schools.

In secondary schools, competition may be more severe because the total number of teachers needed is not likely to change. However, shortages are likely in fields where education graduates have the option of entering another occupation, such as mathematics and the physical sciences.

One further point must be stressed with regard to the outlook for employment. The above paragraphs concern national trends. Local conditions differ. Even though the total number of elementary school teachers will rise, declines are still possible in certain northeastern and other local areas where overall population is declining. Growth is likely to be fastest in the Southwest.

Where to learn more. Contact your local school district and state department of education and other districts or states where you might wish to work to learn the precise requirements for certification in the subjects you wish to teach.

Many teachers are members of associations and unions such as the following:

American Federation of Teachers
555 New Jersey Avenue NW
Washington, DC 20001

National Education Association of the United States
1201 16th Street NW
Washington, DC 20036

A list of accredited schools of education is available from the following association:

National Council for Accreditation of Teacher Education
2029 K Street NW, Ste. 500
Washington, DC 20006

COOKS

Institutional cooks prepare food in large quantities. As they gain experience, they also order food and other supplies, keep records, and supervise kitchen helpers.

Their day might start very early, so they can prepare breakfasts; or run late, so they can clean up after dinner; weekend work is also required for some jobs. Most institutional cooks in government, however, work in elementary and secondary schools, where few breakfasts and no suppers are served; these cooks work only on school days.

Cooks are subject to extreme heat from ovens, steam from boiling pots or dishwashers, and cold from walk-in refrigerators. They are on their feet much of the time.

What you should bring to this occupation. Cooks should have a good sense of taste and smell. They must be able to plan their day carefully so that meals will be ready at the proper time.

A high school diploma is sufficient for most entry-level positions, although some employers prefer new workers who have earned an associate's degree with courses in subjects such as food preparation or menu planning. Experience working in an institutional or restaurant kitchen is likely to impress an employer more than education, however. A health certificate may be required to screen out people with contagious diseases. New workers are usually trained on the job.

The rewards. Cooks have the satisfaction of seeing a job through from beginning to end. Not always having the best quality material to work with because of the need to keep the average cost per meal low may be frustrating. In 1988, average weekly earnings for all cooks except short-order cooks were $241.50. Cooks enjoy the usual fringe benefits.

Where to find a job. This is a fairly large occupation, employing almost 300,000 people in state and local governments. The major employers by far are schools. Hospitals also employ institutional cooks, as do nursing homes, child-care services, and jails and prisons. Employment growth in state and local governments will depend most upon growth of the elementary school population and the growth of hospital employment.

Where to learn more. The following associations may be helpful:

Educational Foundation of the National Restaurant Association
250 S. Wacker Drive #1400
Chicago, IL 60606

American School Food Service Association
1600 Duke Street, 7th Floor
Alexandria, VA 22314

OTHER EDUCATION OCCUPATIONS

Athletic coaches teach individuals and groups how to play different sports and how to improve their performance. They also may select team members, purchase equipment, and organize events. High school coaches usually have teaching duties as well. They must therefore be certified teachers, most often in physical education. Their salaries are comparable with those of other teachers. This is a small occupation, employing only 16,000 people in state and local government. Little change in employment is likely between now and 1995. Competition is usually keen. To learn more about this occupation, you can contact unions or associations such as the National Association for Sport and Physical Education, 1900 Association Drive, Reston, VA 22091.

College professors teach, conduct research, and perform administrative duties. The proportion of time spent on any one activity varies. College teachers are responsible for specialized subjects, the degree of specialization increasing with the size of the school and its involvement with graduate education. A master's degree is sufficient for some positions; the Ph.D. is usually preferred and often required, however. The average salary for college professors in 1988–89 in public institutions was $50,420 for 9 months. Salaries are lower than the average for the occupation in fine and liberal arts; they are higher in engineering, mathematics and some other scientific fields. Total employment is projected to decline between now and 1995. The outlook is complicated by the high degree of specialization required; faculty members trained in one discipline are not qualified to teach in another. As a result, colleges may be unable to find enough teachers for certain subjects, such as engineering, while job hunters cannot find any openings in another field.

Counselors in schools help students deal with personal or family problems, choose courses, and decide what they will do after graduation. They work closely with teachers, school nurses, and school psychologists. School counselors usually have one to five years of education after college. Teaching experience is usually, but not always, required. The average annual salary in 1988–89 was $32,244, according to the Educational Research Service. About 124,000 counselors worked in public schools in 1989. Because much of the employment is concentrated in the secondary schools, little growth is likely to occur between now and 1995. Positions will become available because of turnover, however. To learn more you can contact the American Association for Counseling and Development, 5999 Stevenson Avenue, Alexandria, VA 22304.

Counselors work in many settings other than schools, such as job service offices and social services agencies. Information on these positions is also available from the association listed above.

Speech pathologists work with people who have trouble speaking because of a problem such as a cleft palate, a lisp, or a stutter. They diagnose the problem and plan a course of action, such as teaching the person new ways to use their lips. A master's degree in speech-language pathology is usually required for these workers, although a bachelor's degree is sufficient in some cases. A teaching certificate or certificate to practice speech-language pathology may also be required. In 1983, according to the American Speech-Language-Hearing Association, those with four to six years experience had average salaries of $27,400; those with 16 or more years experience earned $36,900, on average. This is a relatively small occupation with a total employment of less than 50,000 in 1989; state and local government employment was under 30,000 that year, primarily in the schools. Other employers are clinics and hospitals. The occupation is projected to grow as fast as average between now and 1995. To learn more you can contact the American Speech-Language-Hearing Association, 10801 Rockville Pike, Rockville, MD 20852.

Teacher aides assist teachers by taking care of clerical and housekeeping tasks and also help with instruction by working with individual students or small groups. A high school education is sufficient for some positions, but employers prefer at least some college if the person will work with students on lessons. The average hourly wage was $7.05 for instructional aides in 1988–89, according to the Educational Research Service. Noninstructional aides earned about 25 cents less an hour, according to the Bureau of Labor Statistics. This is a fairly large occupation, employing 682,000 people in 1989. About half these workers were part-time employees, and most worked in the primary grades.

CHAPTER 15

FIRE PROTECTION

Fire protection refers to the work of fire departments: putting out fires, conducting inspections, running fire safety programs, and—in many cases—providing emergency medical assistance. Fire departments employ dispatchers, clerks, fire inspectors, fire marshals, and emergency medical technicians. Naturally, the largest occupation is fire fighter. Government employment in fire protection totaled 290,000 in 1988, most of it in the cities.

FIRE FIGHTERS

How many heroes are there in America? At least 260,000. That's the number of fire fighters employed by state and local governments. Fire fighters are among the most respected employees of local governments. No one questions their courage or the importance of their work.

A fire fighter's main duty is to put out fires, obviously enough. All fire fighters must also be prepared to rescue victims and give first aid.

Fire fighters average a 50-hour week; they also have unusual shifts. Some work 24 hours and then have 48 hours off; others work 10 hours for three days and have 2 days off. Still other variations are possible.

To become a fire fighter, you must usually pass a long series of tests. You begin by submitting an application. If you meet certain minimum qualifications, you will be scheduled to take the first of the tests. Minimum qualifications might include age (usually at least 21 and often no more than 35, although many departments have no upper limit) and residency.

You may have to take as many as five different kinds of tests and different kinds of examinations.

Next comes a test of strength and physical agility. The parts of the test are related to a fire fighter's actual duties. You can learn precisely what tests are given by the departments that you want to work for; practice them.

Interviews are another kind of test. At the interview, experienced fire fighters will ask you a series of questions to learn why you want to enter the occupation and what steps you have taken to prepare for it. The board is less concerned about your specific answers than your attitude and personality; they want to see if you keep calm under pressure, follow instructions, express yourself clearly, and are highly motivated.

Medical examinations for fire fighters are stringent. Learn the exact standards for any department you might want to work for before you even apply. Many companies use the National Fire Protection Association Standard 10001. You can obtain a copy of it from the address below and have your own physician examine you so you'll know if you meet the medical qualifications. Among the disqualifying physical conditions are color blindness, poor vision, heart trouble, and back trouble.

Background investigations are conducted by some fire departments, who check for a criminal record, serious driving violations, and credit problems.

Fire fighters are usually trained by the department after being hired. A few departments have formal apprenticeship programs.

The rewards. Fire fighters receive a great deal of satisfaction from their job, which offers extreme challenges and the immediate reward of saving human lives. Prospective fire fighters should also realize that the risk of injury and even death is ever present.

The average starting salary in 1988 was $19,700 according to the International City Manager Association; the average salary was $26,000. Fire fighters are provided with protective clothing by the department and may receive a uniform or uniform allowance. They generally enjoy the usual fringe benefits. Because of the agility needed to perform their duties, fire fighters often are able to retire early; in some cases, they can retire at half pay after 20 years.

Where to find a job. This is a moderate-size occupation, numbering over 290,000; an additional 60,000 people work as fire officers and inspectors. The number of openings projected is smaller than would be expected for an occupation of this size for two reasons. First, turnover is extremely low, an indication of the high degree of satisfaction fire fighters have with their jobs. Second, only slow growth in employment is projected. Competition for fire fighter positions is usually keen.

Where to learn more. The following organizations can provide career information on fire fighters:

Your local fire department

International Association of Fire Chiefs
1329 18th Street NW
Washington, DC 20036

International Association of Fire Fighters
1750 New York Avenue NW
Washington, DC 20006

ANOTHER FIRE DEPARTMENT OCCUPATION: EMERGENCY MEDICAL TECHNICIANS

Emergency medical technicians (EMT's) may work as dispatchers, ambulance attendants, or paramedics. The paramedics are the most highly trained. Both ambulance and paramedic EMT's give first aid to victims of auto accidents, heart attacks, shootings, and other emergencies. Paramedics are able to give aid that requires more complex medical procedures, such as administering intravenous drugs under the supervision of a physician. Ambulance work requires at least one hundred hours of training in a course approved by the U.S. Department of Transportation; training for paramedics takes from four to six times as long. The average salary of EMT-paramedics employed, by work settings, appears in Table 4. To learn more about this occupation, you can contact the National Association of Emergency Medical Technicians, 9140 Ward Parkway, Kansas City, MO 64114.

Table 4:

Average annual salaries of emergency medical tecnhicians by
work setting, 1988

Employer	Paramedic	EMT–I	EMT–Basic
Mean, all settings	$25,210	$20,220	$19,690
Private ambulance services	22,170	16,670	15,450
Fire departments*	31,960	27,430	27,420
Hospitals	21,190	18,250	13,700

*Most fire department EMT's and paramedics are fire fighters who have completed extra training programs.
Source: Journal of Emergency Medical Services

CHAPTER 16

HEALTH

Health is not just the concern of the hospitals. The public health department is usually responsible for preventing the spread of diseases. To do their job, they employ health and regulatory inspectors as well as health professionals. The inspectors check restaurants, grocery stores, and other public places. The health professionals—mostly nurses—work at clinics giving shots and providing information on pregnancy and common health problems. A clinic or local health department can range in size from hundreds of employees to just a few: public health nurse, sanitarian, and clerical worker. Schools also employ public health nurses. Employment in this category was 310,000 in 1988; state governments employ a little less than half the workers; and counties, about one-fourth of them. Among the agencies in this category are public health agencies, mental health agencies, maternity and child care programs, immunization programs, communicable disease programs, and environmental health programs.

PUBLIC HEALTH NURSES

Many public health nurses work to prevent illness by providing information, health screening, and medications such as vaccines. Public health nurses also care for the injured and ill, either in a clinic or as visiting nurses.

Public health nurses usually work a 40-hour week. Evening hours are required at some clinics. Nurses in schools work mostly when the schools are open.

Conditions in clinics and schools are similar in that both are indoors and have ready access to medical supplies. Visiting nurses encounter much more varied conditions and must travel throughout the day despite the weather.

What you should bring to this occupation. Public health nurses must be able to care for all types of people and make sound decisions in the midst of an emergency. More than average stamina may be needed, especially by visiting nurses.

A license is required of fully qualified public health nurses. To obtain the license, a bachelor of science degree in nursing is usually required. Degree programs usually take four to five years; they should not be confused with associate programs that usually take two years. People with associate's degrees may complete the requirements to become registered nurses but not fully qualified public health nurses in most cases.

The rewards. The satisfaction of public health nursing, like that of other nursing fields, is helping to make people well. Public health nurses also enjoy greater independence on the job than most nurses do. Like other nurses, public health nurses must accept the reality of chronic illness and death.

In 1989, the median salary was $31,000, according to the National League for Nursing; the median for school nurses was $28,000.

Where to find a job. Nurses held approximately 1,577,000 jobs in 1988. Many worked for local governments in public and community health agencies. Other major employers are local health departments and clinics. Three percent of all registered nurses worked in schools.

Nursing is a rapidly growing occupation. The combination of fast growth and large size means that many thousands of jobs should become available between now and the year 2000.

Where to learn more.

American Public Health Association, Inc.
1015 15th Street NW
Washington, DC 20005

American School Health Association
7263 State Rte. 43, Box 708
Kent, OH 44240

HEALTH INSPECTORS

Rats, roaches, and rancid cheese are among the less pleasant things in the world; health inspectors try to keep them among the less common. Inspectors usually specialize. *Consumer safety inspectors* check up on food, drugs, and other products, or weights and measures. For example, they might look for mislabeled packages or signs of decomposition or contamination in a product. *Food inspectors* work with veterinarians at meat packing plants, insuring that the animals and the plant meet state standards. *Environmental health inspectors* or *sanitarians* also check some processing plants, such as dairies, but they also ensure that restaurants, hospitals, and other places that serve food are kept clean and free of vermin. They must also do field work and write reports.

Inspectors usually work a standard 40-hour week. Much of their time is spent at inspection sites, working either alone or as part of a team.

What you should bring to this occupation. Inspectors must be able to accept responsibility for their decisions, which can have serious consequences. On the one hand, the duties of their work can close down a business; on the other hand, failure to enforce health codes can result in illness or death. Inspectors must be experts in the field they are going to work in, and they must get along well with a wide range of people under somewhat difficult circumstances.

The education required depends on the specialty. Sanitarians must usually have a bachelor's degree in environmental health or a physical or biological science.

Most states require that environmental health inspectors or sanitarians be licensed.

Employers train new workers in the laws that concern their work and departmental procedures.

The rewards. Inspectors have the satisfaction of contributing to the health of their communities. The constant need to attend to minute details and the possibility of confrontations with restaurant owners or others can be stressful, however.

According to the International Personnel Management Association, average annual earnings for sanitarians employed by cities and counties were $26,700 in 1988; the average earnings for state employees and supervisors were higher.

Where to find a job. About 39,000 health and regulatory inspectors worked for state governments in 1988; 26,000 worked for local governments. City and county health departments are major employers at the local level.

Relatively slow growth is projected for these occupations through 1995; furthermore, turnover is quite low. As a result, the number of jobs available will not be very great.

Where to learn more. The following associations can provide further information about this occupation:

Food Sanitation Institute of the Environmental Management Association
255 Detroit Street, Ste. 200
Denver, CO 80206

International Association of Milk, Food and Environmental Sanitarians, Inc.
502 E. Lincoln Way
Ames, IA 50010–6666

HOMEMAKER-HOME HEALTH AIDES

Home health aides, also sometimes called "homemakers," will become a bigger and bigger category of workers in the coming decade. By all indicators, the older population will continue to increase and will need home health and homemaking services in increasing amounts. In addition, as the cost of health care skyrockets, more patients will be treated in the home to try to control those costs. Further, new technology will make home care increasingly possible. For example, portable versions of machines, formerly only available in-hospital, are already in use in the home. For further information about this rapidly growing field, write to The National Association for Home Care, 519 C Street NE, Washington, DC 20002.

CHAPTER 17

HIGHWAY AND STREET CONSTRUCTION AND MAINTENANCE

Highways, streets, bridges, tunnels, and street lighting systems are built and maintained by state and local governments, even if—as is the case with the interstate system—90 percent of the money to pay for the road comes from the federal government. Civil engineers and surveyors plan the roads, construction workers—many of them heavy equipment operators—build them, construction inspectors—whose duties are described in the chapter on housing—check them while they are being built, large crews of maintenance workers keep them smooth and free of snow, and toll collectors take in some of the money to pay for them. Since much of the construction and maintenance work must be done in the summer, highway departments often hire large numbers of summer workers.

About half a million workers—a little less than 5 percent of all state and local government workers—are in this category; state governments employ about half the workers, and cities and counties divide the rest between them. Employment has been declining in this function of government. A need for major reconstruction and renovation might lead to larger highway departments, but that remains to be seen.

CIVIL ENGINEERS

Civil engineering concerns the design of roads, bridges, and other structures. Civil engineers must determine whether the site is suitable for the structure, what materials are needed, and how much the construction will cost. They also supervise construction. Much of their time is spent writing or delivering reports and consulting with other people working on the project. Specialists within this occupation include structural engineers, highway engineers, construction engineers, hydraulic engineers, traffic engineers, and soil mechanics engineers.

Engineers generally work a 40-hour week, mostly in a comfortable office, although travel to construction sites is also necessary.

What you should bring to this occupation. Engineers need good math and verbal skills, and they also must work well with other people.

The standard educational requirement for civil engineers is a bachelor of civil engineering degree. The course of study includes subjects such as physics, calculus, surveying, structural mechanics, and the mechanics of fluids.

The rewards. The turnover rate for engineers is quite low, indicating that employed engineers prefer keeping their present jobs to finding new ones.

Engineers are among the highest paid workers. Other engineering specialties pay even better than civil engineering on average. In 1989, the average starting salary for civil engineers reported by the College Placement Council was $25,600. Overall, the average salary for civil engineers in 1989 was between $35,000 and $46,000, according to the American Management Association. Engineers have the usual fringe benefits.

Where to find a job. About 48,000 civil engineers work for state and local governments. The major employers are highway and public works departments.

Civil engineering is projected to grow 47 percent by 1995, which is faster than average.

Where to learn more. Career information is available from the following associations:

American Society of Civil Engineers
345 East 47th Street
New York, NY 10017

Education Foundation
  American Public Works Association
  1313 East 60th Street
  Chicago, Il 60637

Society of Women Engineers
  345 East 47th, Room 305
  New York, NY 10017

OTHER HIGHWAY AND CONSTRUCTION OCCUPATIONS

Heavy equipment operators are also known as construction machinery operators or operating engineers. They drive bulldozers, backhoes, paving machines, and other equipment. They usually have experience as construction laborers or helpers before becoming heavy equipment operators. Average weekly earning in 1989 was $610. Operators employed by state and local governments are less affected by unemployment than are most construction workers. Employment in state and local governments in 1989 was 91,000. To learn more about this occupation, contact the International Union of Operating Engineers, 1125 17th Street NW, Washington, DC 20036.

Highway maintenance workers have a great many duties. Signs and lines must be painted, potholes filled, cracks patched, grass mown, and snow plowed. A high school education is usually required. In 1989, the hourly wage ranged from $10 to $16. This is a moderate-size occupation, employing 185,000 workers in 1989, all of them with state and local governments, which are the major employers. To learn more about this occupation, you can visit the Job Service, which has job listings and offers employment counseling. You can also contact the American Federation of State, County and Municipal Employees, 1625 L Street NW, Washington, DC 20001.

CHAPTER 18

HOUSING AND COMMUNITY DEVELOPMENT

When the first European settlers landed at Jamestown, in what is now Virginia, the community's first concern was housing. Housing is still a concern of local governments, whether the government has a housing authority that builds and operates developments or simply has a building standards agency, planning commission, or zoning board. Although housing is a fairly major function of state and local government, it is a minor function in terms of employment; fewer than 160,000 people worked in it in 1988, all of them for local governments.

CONSTRUCTION INSPECTORS

Although what goes up must come down, construction inspectors make sure that a building will not collapse before its time. They are highly specialized, some dealing with public works and others with buildings. Public works inspectors are further categorized by special areas such as highways, streets, bridges, tunnels, dams, and sewer and water systems. Specialities within building inspection include structural, electrical, and mechanical, which concern plumbing, gas lines, and heating systems.

Inspectors usually check on a project more than once during construction to ensure that it conforms with building codes.

Inspectors keep records of their work and write reports. They usually work a standard 40-hour week, spending about half their time in the office and half at construction sites.

What you should bring to this occupation. Knowledge of the principals of good construction and attention to detail characterize construction inspectors. They must also know the law and be able to communicate. They must usually have experience as a contractor, supervisor, or craftperson. People who have completed an apprenticeship, studied engineering or architecture for two years, or earned an associate's degree in a relevant subject are preferred. This is not a job for beginning workers.

The rewards. Successful building inspectors enjoy the complexity of the work and the challenge of working with a great variety of people. The job offers more security than other construction related occupations, but does not provide the satisfaction of actually building something.

The average salary for construction inspectors with state and local governments was $25,700 in 1988.

Where to find a job. This is a fairly small occupation, with 54,000 state and local government employees. Construction inspectors usually work for the building, public works, engineering, or maintenance department of the local government. Those with the state government are most likely to be with the highway department.

Only slow growth is projected for this occupation and turnover is low. Opportunities are best in rapidly growing communities or states.

Where to learn more. Local governments and the following associations can provide more information about the job of construction inspector:

International Conference of Building Officials
5360 South Workman Mill Road
Whittier, CA 90601

Building Officials and Code Administrations International, Inc.
4051 Flossmoor Road
Country Club Hills, IL 60477–5795

URBAN PLANNERS

Urban and regional planners design new or renovated developments. Also known as community or city planners, they juggle the need for housing, schools, industrial sites, business sections, and parks along with requirements for transportation, sanitation, electricity, and natural gas. They must study current conditions, consider long-term development, estimate costs, build models, present plans before authorizing boards, and supervise construction. A master's degree in planning is the usual educational requirement, although some positions require only a bachelor's degree. In 1988, average salaries for planners with local governments were $32,000; planners with state governments averaged $38,000. This is a relatively small occupation with a total employment of 21,000 in 1989; local, regional, and state government planning commissions employ about 60 percent of these workers. Only slow growth is projected between now and 1995. To learn more about this occupation, you can contact the American Planning Association, 1776 Massachusetts Avenue, NW, Washington, DC 20036.

CHAPTER 19

HOSPITALS

Hospitals employ some of the best-paid workers in the country—doctors—and some of the poorest-paid—nursing aides and orderlies. In between come a host of other people: clinical laboratory technicians, general clerks, hospital administrators, kitchen helpers, licensed practical nurses, medical laboratory technologists, registered nurses, psychiatric aides, radiological technicians, and secretaries. They employ at least 50,000 workers in each of those categories. The operation of public hospitals is the largest single function of state and local governments after education. State and local government employment in hospitals exceeded 1 million in 1988; about half the employment was at the state level. In addition, they are the major place of employment for many other technicians, technologists, and therapists. Most of these occupations are growing faster than average.

About half the hospitals in the country are public. Local hospitals are often general hospitals, which means they care for all sorts of injuries and illnesses. About 240 state hospitals are long-term psychiatric hospitals, serving the retarded and mentally ill. A trend toward smaller, residential facilities, group homes, and other less restricted environments for these patients has reduced the staffs of these hospitals, although they still employ more than 200,000 people.

REGISTERED NURSES

The needs of the patient, and the instructions of the patient's doctor determine most of the duties of the nurse. Nurses give people shots, test blood pressure, and bandage wounds, keeping records of everything they do. Some nurses spend their day caring for bedridden patients who, besides medical care, need help with eating and with personal hygiene. Other nurses are primarily concerned with supervising orderlies, nurse aides, licensed practical nurses, and technicians.

Hours and working conditions for nurses vary. Nursing care must be provided 24 hours a day, so many nurses work nights and weekends. Although an 8-hour, 5-day week is still fairly standard, it is not universal. Many nurses work 10 hours a day for 4 days and then have 3 days off, for example. The proportion of nurses who work part-time (28 percent) is much higher than for most occupations that require so much education and training.

The actual working conditions of a nurse depend a great deal on the kinds of patients being cared for. Emergency rooms, nurseries, orthopedic wards, and intensive care units, for example, are very different places. All nurses, however, may suddenly be confronted with life-threatening situations.

What you should bring to this occupation. Nursing requires emotional stability and physical stamina. Nurses need good communication skills so that they can explain what they are doing to patients.

The educational requirements for *registered nurses* have been the subject of controversy for the past 10 years. Three different kinds of programs enable prospective nurses to take the required licensing exam. Programs in community colleges that last about 2 to 3 years and lead to an associate's degree now train about 45 percent of the new registered nurses. Programs connected to hospitals that last 2 to 3 years and lead to a nursing diploma now train about 8 percent. Programs run by colleges or universities that last 4 to 5 years and lead to a Bachelor of Science Degree in Nursing (B.S.N.) now train the balance, about 47 percent.

While graduates of all three types of programs usually qualify for positions as staff nurses, each program has its advantages. The shortest programs are much less expensive both in terms of cost and—even more important—in terms of lost income while you are being trained. Hospital programs are often said to provide more practice working with patients. And B.S.N. degrees are required for public health nursing, admission to graduate school, and some supervisory positions. Graduates of 2- and 3-year programs may go back to school and earn a B.S.N., but the school may require that they retake several courses, adding to the time and expense of their education.

The rewards. Many nurses receive great satisfaction from helping the sick or injured become well. Their duties are not always pleasant, of course, direct patient care can be very hard work. Another difficulty with being a nurse is that not all the patients get better.

In 1988, the average salary of staff nurses working in government hospitals ranged from $27,000 to $33,000, according to the American Management Association. Nurses receive the usual fringe benefits.

Nurses can advance in two ways, by taking on more supervisory responsibilities or by earning a graduate degree and certification that enables them to provide a higher level of nursing care, such as a nurse practitioner, nurse anesthetist, or clinical nurse.

Where to find a job. About 646,000 registered nurses worked for state and local governments in 1988; an additional 886,000 worked for other employers. Hospitals, public and private, employ more than 65 percent of all nurses. Other major employers are nursing homes (most of which are privately operated), public health departments, physicians' offices, and schools.

The number of people in nursing is projected to grow almost 50 percent by 1995. Even more jobs will become available because of turnover. Nursing shortages exist, especially in some rural areas and in some special fields. According to the U.S. Department of Labor job openings for nurses are expected to grow much faster than average through the year 2000.

Where to learn more. Information about a career as a registered nurse is available from these organizations:

Career Information Services National League for Nursing
350 Hudson Street
New York, NY 10014

American Nurses' Association
2420 Pershing Road
Kansas City, MO 64108

American Hospital Association
Division of Nursing
840 North Lake Shore Drive
Chicago, IL 60611

OTHER HOSPITAL OCCUPATIONS

Clinical laboratory technicians are often known by their specialities; for example, they may be called medical laboratory technologists or technicians, blood-bank specialists, or biochemistry technicians. In general, these workers perform chemical and other kinds of tests on body fluids and tissues, such as the measurement of the amount of cholesterol in a blood sample. Some of these jobs require an associate's degree; others—those for technologists—require a bachelor of science degree. The average salary for clinical laboratory technicians was $20,000 in 1989, according to the Bureau of Labor Statistics. Medical laboratory technicians in government had median annual salaries ranging from $20,000 to $22,500 in 1988, depending on the size of the hospital, according to the American Management Association. This is a moderate-size occupation; total employment in these fields was 242,000 in 1989. The occupations are growing faster than average, and turnover makes *many thousands of jobs available each* year. To learn more about this occupation, you can contact the American Society for Medical Technology, 2021 L Street NW, Ste. 400, Washington, DC 20036.

Hospital administrators—who are also known as *health services administrators*—are responsible for seeing that the medical staff has the equipment, working conditions, and personnel needed to treat the patients. Budgeting finances, hiring personnel, keeping the physical plant in shape, coordinating departments, and training the staff all come under their direction. Most hospital administrators have a master's degree in health care administration, although a bachelor's degree in business and management is sufficient for some positions. Administrators usually start as assistants. According to the American Management Association, the average salary in government hospitals ranged from $45,000 to $80,000 in 1989, increasing with the size of the hospitals. Assistant administrators earned $34,000 to $48,000 that year in government hospitals. Besides hospitals and health departments, health services administrators also work for nursing homes, clinics, health maintenance organizations, and group practices. To learn more contact unions or associations such as: American College of Healthcare Executives, 840 North Lake Shore Drive, Chicago, IL 60611; Association of University Programs in Health Administration, 1911 Fort Myer Drive, Suite 503, Arlington, VA 22209; National Health Council, Health Career Programs, 350 Fifth Avenue, Ste. 1118, New York, NY 10018.

Licensed practical nurses (LPN's) provide bedside care; they bathe patients, give massages, and change dressings. They also check the patient's vital signs—temperature, blood pressure, pulse, and respiration. Under supervision, they may administer medications. To become an LPN, you must complete a one-year training program in a vocational school or community college. Average salaries for LPN's are in the lower third for all wage earners; the average annual salary, depending on the size of the hospital, in 1988 ranged from $14,700 to $21,200 in government hospitals, according to the American Management Association. This is a fairly large occupation, employing 626,000 in 1988; more than half these workers were employed by hospitals. Other major employers are nursing homes and physicians' offices. Between now and 1995, fast growth combined with turnover should make thousands of jobs available each year. To learn more about this occupation, you can contact unions or associations such as: National League for Nursing, 350 Hudson Street, New York, NY 10014; National Federation of Licensed Practical Nurses, Inc., P.O. Box 18088, Raleigh, NC 27619.

Nurse aides and orderlies take care of many of the patients' basic needs. They make beds, feed, bathe, dress, and transport patients, and set up equipment. High school graduates are usually preferred for these jobs, but a high school diploma is not always required. This is one of the lowest paid occupations in the country. According to the American Management Association, as of 1988, earnings were often only a little above the minimum wage, averaging $11,900 in government hospitals, depending on the size of the hospital. This is a very large occupational group, employing 1.8 million people in 1989; state and local government employment, which is concentrated in hospitals, exceeded 300,000 that year. The occupation is projected to grow faster than average between now and 1995. Turnover is high. This combination means that many thousands of jobs will become available each year.

Physicians work to prevent illness, restore health, and repair the results of injuries. Some treat the whole person, but most specialize in particular parts of the body, such as the heart or brain. They are among the most thoroughly educated workers, the course of study taking from four to ten years after college, including both medical school and residency requirements. They are also among the best paid, with an average income of $160,000 after expenses in 1991. Median salaries for hospital interns were $19,800; and median salaries for emergency-room physicians were $89,000. This is a fairly large occupation; 535,000 doctors were working in 1988. Most are self-employed. In 1989, state and local government employment of doctors was 73,000. To learn more about this occupation, you can contact associations such as: Council on Medical Education, American Medical Association, 515 North State Street, Chicago, IL 60610.

Psychiatric aides work with the mentally and emotionally ill usually in hospitals and other health care facilities. They help patients with personal hygiene, if necessary, and encourage them to join in group or recreational activities. A high school education is preferred though not always required. Salaries are comparable to those of nurse aides, which are among the lower third for all wage earners. This is a moderate-size occupation, employing about 114,000 people. The occupation is projected to grow at an average rate through the year 2000. To learn more about this occupation contact National Mental Health Association, 1021 Prince Street, Alexandria, VA 22314–2971.

Therapist is a general title for a worker in the health field who helps people overcome physical or emotional difficulties. Specialties within this group are highly specific; a worker trained in one of them is not qualified to work in another one. Among the titles of job specialties are physical, occupational, speech, recreation, art, dance, music, and horticultural therapist; rehabilitation counselor; audiologist; and orientation therapist for the blind. Some therapists diagnose the person's problem and devise ways to conquer it; others work in cooperation with a doctor who diagnoses and prescribes treatment. They usually need at least a bachelor's degree in their specialized field. Salaries ranged in 1988 from $25,000 to $33,400.

CHAPTER 20

LIBRARY

Librarians in public libraries usually work for local governments, who employed about 143,000 workers in this category in 1988. Librarians almost always need a bachelor's degree and often a master's. More libraries are operated by the schools; these librarians may be required to be former teachers as well as having additional education. Many libraries also employ *library aides,* however, who do not need as much education.

LIBRARIANS

Video cassettes, phonograph records, film strips, books—today, information comes in many forms. Librarians must be familiar with them all, for their job is to make information available. Some librarians perform technical services—ordering books, cataloging material, or having sets of magazines bound for the permanent collection. Most librarians provide user services. They explain how the library is arranged, where different kinds of material are kept, and how to use machines such as microfilm and microfiche readers. The majority of librarians work in schools; teaching students how to use a library is an important part of their duties.

Librarians usually work a 5-day, 40-hour week. Depending on the hours the library is open, evening or weekend work may be required. Many librarians—more than 20 percent—work part time.

What you should bring to this occupation. Successful librarians are good at explaining things to a great variety of people. Librarians also need good memories for the sources of information.

Schools often prefer to hire former teachers who have taken additional education related to library science, media resources, or audiovisual communications. Public libraries prefer applicants who have earned a master of library science degree.

The rewards. Librarians have the satisfaction of helping people find what they need. Librarians express some dissatisfaction with their wages, which are quite low for the education required.

Librarians can advance into administrative positions, some of which require additional education. School librarians have fewer opportunities to become supervisors since there is often only one librarian in the school.

Starting salaries of librarians in public libraries who had a master of library science degree were $21,531 in 1988. School librarians had average starting salaries of $25,183 in 1988–89, according to the Educational Research Service.

Where to find a job. About 130,000 librarians worked for state and local governments in 1989, mostly in schools and public libraries. More than 70 percent of all librarians are in the educational services sector, whereas less than 11 percent work in public libraries.

Employment growth in school libraries should be similar to that for teachers; this would mean that growth is likely in the elementary schools, and decline is probable in the universities between now and 1995. The employment of librarians in public libraries is projected to grow more slowly than average between now and 1995, but employment in specialized libraries will continue to grow.

The following associations have information on this career:

American Library Association
50 East Huron Street
Chicago, IL 60611

National Education Association of the United States
1201 16th Street NW
Washington, DC 20036

LIBRARY TECHNICIANS AND AIDES

Library technicians and aides (who may also be called assistants, helpers, or clerks) perform a variety of duties that help a library run smoothly. They check books and other materials in and out, sort and shelve them, calculate fines, locate items for users, issue library cards, repair or bind materials, and provide information. Technicians have more complicated duties and less supervision than aides. Some college coursework (up to two years in a program for technicians) may be required of technicians; a high school education is usually sufficient for aides. Aides with simple clerical duties receive salaries comparable to other clerical workers. To learn more about this occupation, you can contact the Council on Library-Media-Technicians-Assistants, Cuyahoga Community College, Attn: Margaret R. Barron, 2900 Community College Avenue, Cleveland, Ohio 44115.

CHAPTER 21

NATURAL RESOURCES

Natural resources are managed by state and local governments and by federal agencies such as the Department of Agriculture and Department of the Interior. The state agency will be called the Department of Public Resources, Department of Conservation, or other similar name. Among the functions of the state and local agencies—which employ about 190,000 people—are agricultural extension and inspection services, fish stocking, flood control, forest fire prevention and control, irrigation, land and forest reclamation, mineral resource management, and soil conservation. State and local government employment in natural resources was 190,000 in 1988. Most of the employment is at the state level, although counties and special districts also have some workers in this category.

Workers include agricultural extension agents, foresters, range managers, and fish and game wardens.

FORESTERS

Foresters are doctors for the woods. Their goal is to ensure that the trees are healthy and protected from disease, fire, and infestations of insects. They pursue this goal in many ways, including conducting research, supervising parks, managing watersheds, replanting burned over or harvested forests, and establishing guidelines for lumbering operations. Foresters usually work eight hours a day, five days a week.

Much of their work takes place in offices, but they may be required to work outside in all kinds of weather, especially if a forest fire is raging or a hiking party gets lost.

What you should bring to this occupation. Foresters generally have an aptitude for science and enough physical agility to make their way in the woods. A bachelor's degree in forestry is required for most entry-level positions, and a graduate degree is often preferred. The college curriculum includes courses in forest protection and silviculture; frequently, a summer camp that provides practical experience is required.

The rewards. Foresters receive satisfaction from working to preserve the woods or to make them more productive. Competition for these jobs has been extreme for some time, however, and relocating is often necessary to find employment.

The average salary for foresters employed by state governments ranged from $14,000 to $32,000 in 1988.

Where to find a job. This is a fairly small occupation, totaling 30,000 in 1988, of whom half work for the federal government and only 10,000 for state and local governments. Lumber companies are the principal employers of foresters outside the government.

Only slow growth is projected for this occupation and turnover is low. These factors, combined with the small number employed to begin with, indicate that relatively few jobs will be available through 1995.

Where to learn more. The following organizations can provide further information about forestry:

Society of American Foresters
5400 Grosvenor Lane
Bethesda, MD 20814

American Forestry Association
1516 P Street NW
Washington, DC 20005

OTHER NATURAL RESOURCES OCCUPATIONS

Extension agents, who are also known as agricultural or home economics extension agents, are teachers without classrooms. They work with individuals and groups to spread information about agriculture and home economics. Specialties include horticulture, grain crops, animal husbandry, disease and insect control, nutrition, human relations, child development, and consumer education. Extension agents also direct 4H activities and write articles on their specialties. The job requires at least a bachelor's degree in agriculture or home economics. In 1988, the starting salaries were about $20,000 and top salaries exceeded $30,000. This is a small occupation, employing only 14,000 in 1988. Additional jobs are available for paraprofessionals. The extension service is a joint endeavour of the federal, state, and county governments, but the employer is the state government, usually the land grant university (of which the service is an extension). To learn more about this occupation, you can contact your local agent, the state university that operates the service, or the Extension Office, Science and Education Administration, U.S. Department of Agriculture, Washington, DC 20250.

Fish and game wardens make sure that hunters, trappers, anglers, and commercial fishermen obey game laws. Much of their time is spent on routine patrols, but they also investigate complaints and make reports on wildlife. A high school education is usually required. The salary range in 1988 was from $16,000 to $19,500, according to TSC. This is a small occupation, employing only several thousand people. State governments are the major employers, although the federal government and some local governments also employ a few wardens.

CHAPTER 22

PARKS AND RECREATION

Parks operated by state and local governments range in size from small playgrounds to vast forests. Besides playgrounds, a park department may also run pools, public beaches, golf courses, museums, botanical gardens, and zoos, each of which needs different kinds of workers. In parks and recreation, state and local governments employed 280,000 workers in 1988; cities employed about 100,000 of the workers; states and counties employed most of the rest. The Department of Interior's National Park Service is responsible for most federal parks.

All parks need administrative and maintenance workers. City parks often have special programs and employ recreation workers trained to run such activities. Lifeguards, gardeners, animal keepers, and museum technicians are some of the other people who work for parks departments.

PARK RANGERS

Park rangers are responsible for maintaining order in public parks, which involves directing traffic, providing information, and patrolling the park to prevent violations of the law or park rules. Administering first aid and assisting with disabled vehicles are common tasks.

Park rangers are outdoors in all kinds of weather. They usually work a 40-hour week, but their shifts are irregular. Since the parks are busiest on weekends and holidays, rangers are likely to work then.

What you should bring to this occupation. Park rangers must be able to keep calm in emergencies, make decisions rapidly, and remain courteous after the two hundredth repetition of the same question.

A high school education is usually required; college-level courses in recreational leadership, environmental science, psychology, sociology, and biology may be helpful.

Applicants are given a series of tests before becoming ranger trainees, including written exams, physical agility tests, medical examinations, and interviews. Rangers are trained after being hired, sometimes at a police academy.

The rewards. Rangers have the satisfaction of combining an interest in the outdoors with protecting people and the parks.

Rangers will most likely receive salaries comparable to those of police officers in the same area.

Where to find a job. This is a relatively small occupation, employing about 18,000 people. In various states, agencies that employ rangers might be called any of the following names: Department of Parks; Department of Parks and Recreation; Department of Natural Resources; Department of Conservation; Department of Forests and Waters; and even, in Delaware, the Highway Department.

OTHER PARKS AND RECREATION OCCUPATIONS

Landscape architects design gardens and parks. They determine which plants are suitable for an area, taking the soil, sunlight, water supply, and proposed use into account. They also plan the type and position of roads, walks, fences, lamps, furniture, drains, and sprinkler systems. A bachelor's degree in landscape architecture—which may take five years to complete—is usually required. In 1988, the average salary was $37,000, according to a survey of members of the American Society of Landscape Architects. This is a small occupation, with 19,000 workers in 1988. The major employers in state and local government are park departments, school systems, hospitals, city planning agencies, and extension services. To learn more about this occupation, contact the American Society of Landscape Architects, 1733 Connecticut Avenue NW, Washington, DC 20009.

Lifeguards are primarily responsible for preventing drownings or other accidents at pools and beaches. They may also teach people to swim, clean the pool, and check the chlorine level of the water. Red Cross Lifeguard Certification is usually required. Applicants for certification must demonstrate the ability to swim and dive to specific degrees, and to rescue swimmers; CPR or other types of training may also be required. The training for lifeguards is extensive and has been standardized primarily by the Red Cross. Two certifications are the most common: the Advanced Life Saving Certificate and the Water Safety Instructor Certificate. The average salary for lifeguards is in the lower third for all wage earners; hourly wages of $8 or less were reported in 1988. Hiring for these positions, most of which are seasonal, frequently begins in January. To learn more about this occupation, contact the U.S. Lifesaving Association, c/o Chicago Park District, 425 E. 14th Boulevard, Chicago, IL 60605.

Recreation workers organize games and other activities to help people make the most of their free time. The kinds of activities they direct depend in part on the place where they work, which can range in size from a city playground to a vast forest. A bachelor's degree is usually required; for some positions, the degree must be in recreation and leisure studies or a special field such as music or art. In 1988, the average salary for recreation workers employed by state governments was $18,100; local government employees averaged $17,200. This is a moderate-size occupation with a total employment of 186,000 in 1988; state and local government employment was 62,000. To learn more about this occupation, contact the following: National Recreation and Park Association, Division of Professional Services, 3101 Park Center Drive, Alexandria VA 22302; American Association for Leisure and Recreation, 1900 Association Drive, Reston, VA 22091.

CHAPTER 23

POLICE

Police protection is largely a task of the local government, with no function other than education employing so many city workers. In 1988, state and local government employment in police protection was 682,000; of that number, 52,000 worked for state governments, 190,000 for counties, and 440,000 for cities. Police officers investigate crimes, arrest suspects, and direct traffic. In large cities, individual police officers usually specialize in one kind of work. In small towns, they do a little bit of everything. Much of the work is routine, but some people are attracted to the job because a routine patrol can suddenly turn into a hot pursuit.

State police are organized in several different ways. State police departments typically provide full police services for unincorporated areas of the state. Highway patrols chiefly enforce traffic laws and assist motorists who have been in an accident or have other problems. However the distinctions are not always clear. Arizona and Texas, for example, have highway patrols within their state police departments. Hawaii has neither a state police department nor a highway patrol.

Hiring standards and evaluation procedures for state departments are similar to those of city departments.

POLICE OFFICERS

Television and motion picture cops and robbers bear little resemblance to real policemen. Most officers are assigned to patrol or traffic control duties. Boredom is often the norm. Patrolling a neighborhood enables officers to know what activities are normal, so that they can spot the unusual; it also tends to prevent crime. At any time, patrol officers may be called upon to stop a burglary, quiet a disturbance, or save a life. Traffic officers direct traffic, give out tickets, and deal with accidents.

Police departments also have divisions that specialize in investigations of certain types of crimes, such as burglaries or homicides, or in other activities, such as juvenile affairs. Other special units are motorcycle patrols, mobile rescue teams, and helicopter divisions. Officers may also be assigned to crime laboratories, record divisions, or police clerk duties.

No matter what their assignment, police officers spend much of their time completing reports of incidents. These reports can serve to build a case or indicate a problem. They are also needed because another important duty of officers is to testify in court.

Officers usually work 40 hours a week, but not from 9 to 5, Monday to Friday. Police protection must be provided every hour of the day, every day of the year. Consequently, officers work unusual shifts, including most holidays. Furthermore, they are usually on call 24 hours a day in case a sudden emergency arises. Officers must also be prepared to work outdoors in all kinds of weather.

What you should bring to this occupation. Successful police officers, to paraphrase Kipling, can keep their heads when all around them are losing theirs. They are also able both to follow orders and to take charge of a situation. They enjoy working with others.

Many cities have a maximum age limit for job entry of about 35. Most require that applicants be at least 21 years old; some departments hire police cadets, however, who are younger. A high school diploma is almost always required, and some departments look for applicants with at least some college education, often in fields such as law enforcement or the administration of justice.

Prospective police recruits are evaluated in many different ways. A background investigation, medical examination, and interview are almost universal. Psychological evaluation, polygraph testing, physical performance tests, and written tests are also used by many departments.

Interviews are designed to determine whether you are highly motivated and can keep calm under pressure. You should learn exactly what is required and practice for all the different types of tests to learn early if you have any disqualifying conditions.

Training usually begins at a police academy run by the department or the state; academy training lasts six months in New York. It combines physical conditioning and self-defense with the study of law and police procedure. First aid and marksmanship are also learned and practiced. Training continues when a recruit is assigned to a station. And evaluation continues during both training and a probationary period.

The rewards. Police officers experience satisfaction from preventing crimes and ensuring the safety of their fellow citizens. Among the drawbacks of the occupation are that a great deal of paperwork is required, the danger of injury and death is ever present, and the fight against crime is never won.

Police officers advance by being promoted through the ranks. Additional testing usually takes place at every rank. Officers may also become more specialized in their work, concentrating on one type of police activity.

The mean salary in 1988 was $26,700, according to the Bureau of Labor Statistics. According to the International City Management Association, in 1989 the average entrance salary was $20,600, and the average maximum basic salary was $28,000. Officers receive the usual fringe benefits plus a uniform or uniform allowance and required equipment, including weapons. Because of the agility that officers must have, many departments have pension plans that permit an officer to retire after 20 or 25 years of service at half pay.

Where to find a job. More than one half million people work as local police officers and detectives; they are ten times more numerous than state police officers.

These occupations are projected to grow more slowly than average during the next decade, in part because of the use of civilian technicians to perform specialized duties once performed by officers. Turnover is also relatively low for this occupation. However, because of the occupation's size, a great many openings will become available. If the past is any guide, competition for those openings will be keen.

Where to learn more. Your local police department and state police department or highway patrol are the best places to obtain precise information on job requirements, salaries, and test schedules.

Many police officers are members of unions or professional associations such as the following.

Fraternal Order of Police
2100 Gardiner Lane
Louisville, KY 40205–2900

American Federation of Police
3801 Biscayne Boulevard
Miami, FL 33137

National Brotherhood of Police Officers
285 Dorchester
Boston, MA 02127

OTHER POLICE PROTECTION OCCUPATIONS

Crossing guards ensure the safety of children at busy intersections before and after school. A high school diploma is usually required; good character is important, and extensive background checks are often performed. Hourly wages based on the 1990 Census and adjusted for inflation were $9.20 in 1989. For more information, contact a local police department.

Detectives gather evidence for criminal cases. They interview witnesses and suspects, keep watch over suspects, and assist in arrests. Most have several years experience as police officers before becoming detectives. Detectives usually earn more than police officers. Local and state police departments employed about 50,000 detectives in 1988. To learn more about this occupation, consult the sources of information listed under police officers.

Dispatchers who work for police departments, fire departments, and hospitals receive telephone and radio calls from people seeking assistance and broadcast the necessary information to field units. They also keep records, or logs, of the calls they receive and the action they take. A high school education is usually required of these workers and, frequently, an FCC radio license. National salary data are not available for this occupation; any police department can provide local information, however. In 1988, about 54,000 people worked as police, fire, and ambulance dispatchers, making this a relatively small occupation. Local governments employ 90 percent of these workers.

Police clerks perform various clerical tasks to keep the police department functioning smoothly. They keep records, order supplies, run computers, and operate switchboards. A high school diploma is usually required. According to the 1990 Census, about 88,000 people worked as secretaries, typists, file clerks, and record clerks for local governments in justice, public order, and safety. To learn more about this occupation, you should contact local police departments.

Sheriffs combine the duties of a police chief and warden because the county sheriff's department is responsible for traffic control, criminal investigations, and jailing prisoners in the county's jurisdiction. In some states—California, for example—sheriffs also act as coroners. Sheriffs are elected in every state except Rhode Island, where they are appointed. Salaries of sheriffs vary widely, depending upon the size of the county they work for. This is a relatively small occupation, since by definition there can be only one sheriff in a county, no matter how many deputies there are. Deputy sheriffs are grouped with police officers as a vocational category. To learn more about this occupation, consult your local sheriff's office as well as the sources of information described in the appendix.

State highway patrol officers are chiefly responsible for traffic control on major highways. Officers also perform regular police functions in unincorporated parts of a state. In general, officers must meet the same standards as police officers in city departments. Salaries are comparable to those of police officers. Most of the sources of information listed at the end of the section on police officer also have information on state highway patrol officers.

CHAPTER 24

SANITATION

Sanitation is generally the responsibility of the local government, although often, especially in smaller communities, the government contracts with a private company for sanitation services. Still, about 100,000 people work for sanitation departments driving trucks, collecting refuse, and performing other duties. The largest occupation in these departments is sanitation workers.

SANITATION WORKERS

When asked how business was, the sanitation worker replied cheerfully, "It's picking up." Sanitation workers pick up refuse from homes and businesses and burn it or use it for landfill. Jobs include refuse collector, truck driver, incinerator operator, and landfill operator. Many sanitation workers start as refuse collectors either emptying trash cans into a truck or operating special trucks that pick up larger bins and dumpsters.

The standard workweek is 40 hours. Sanitation workers are outside in all kinds of weather, both winter ice and summer heat, making their job more difficult.

What you should bring to this occupation. Sanitation workers should enjoy physical labor and working outside, since lifting heavy cans and walking much of the day is their major job. A high school education is usually required, and applicants may have to be licensed drivers.

The rewards. No one is likely to consider sanitation work a glamorous job; the work must be done, however, and sanitation workers are proud of the contribution they make to the health of their communities.

Sanitation workers start as laborers and can advance to driver and then to supervisory positions. The median wage for experienced collection workers was $16,000 in 1989, according to the International City Management Association.

Where to find a job. State and local governments employ about 90,000 garbage collectors, local governments being the major employers.

Government employment in sanitation declined during the 1980s. Some of the decline is due to greater productivity. Another factor is that more and more governments are hiring contractors to collect refuse and perform other sanitation functions.

Where to learn more. The following unions can provide further information:

American Federation of State, County and Municipal Employees
1625 L Street NW
Washington, DC 20001

International Brotherhood of Teamsters, Chauffeurs,
    Warehousemen and Helpers of America
25 Louisiana Avenue NW
Washington, DC 20001

CHAPTER 25

TRANSPORTATION

Public mass transportation systems include subways, surface railroads, and bus systems. In 1988, state and local government employment in the transit category was 210,000, all but 21,000 of it at the local level. Bus driver is the largest single transit occupation.

BUS DRIVERS

Through rain and snow and gloom of night—not to mention traffic jams—bus drivers daily carry millions of people, mostly schoolchildren. Drivers inspect the bus before starting, checking such things as safety equipment, fuel supply, and brakes. They follow a specified schedule, being careful not to be early or late. Local transit bus drivers also collect fares, issue transfers, and provide route information. Bus drivers must also be able to make out route and accident reports.

A very large number of bus drivers—45 percent—work part time. School bus drivers usually work 20 to 30 hours a week. The standard workweek for local transit bus drivers is 40 hours; however, split shifts, in which the driver is on duty for both the morning and evening rush hours with several hours off in between, are common. Weekend work is also required of local transit bus drivers.

Working conditions for drivers largely depend on the weather, even though the bus provides protection from the elements.

What you should bring to this occupation. Bus drivers should like working with people and being independent at the same time. They should have the patience to deal with noisy children and traffic delays. They should speak well enough to answer a rider's questions.

Applicants should have a driver's license; a chauffeur's license is usually required to drive a bus, but you may be able to obtain the license after being hired. You should learn the policy of the company or transportation authority you wish to work for before applying.

A high school education is preferred, but not always required. Indeed, some school bus drivers are as young as 16, although 18 is the usual minimum age. Local transit bus drivers must usually be at least 21.

A driving test and a medical examination may be required. Some states require a background check of school bus drivers to ensure that applicants do not have a history of emotional instability.

After being hired, drivers are trained for two to eight weeks in practical driver training, traffic laws, and bus company regulations.

The rewards. Successful bus drivers enjoy driving and like being outside and moving around. The job can be stressful, however; opportunities for promotion are limited, and seasonal layoffs may be routine. Drivers may become dispatchers, but few other opportunities for advancement are available.

Average salaries for school bus drivers are much lower than for local transit drivers. In 1988–89, the average hourly wage for school bus drivers was $8.56, according to the Educational Research Service. According to the American Public Transit Association, the median starting salary for local transit bus drivers in 1989 was $9.00 an hour and the median top—which would be reached after 2 or 3 years—was $13.30 in cities of 1 million or more people. Drivers receive the usual fringe benefits.

Where to find a job. The number of school bus drivers—380,000—is very large. Far fewer people—62,000—drive for local transit companies. A driver can tell you where to ask for information.

This occupation is projected to grow slowly through 1995. Even so, openings should be plentiful because of the size of the occupation and because turnover among drivers is above average.

Where to learn more. Many local transit bus drivers are members of unions such as the following.

Amalgamated Transit Union
5025 Wisconsin Avenue NW
Washington, DC 20016

Transport Workers Union of America
80 West End Avenue
New York, NY 10023

International Brotherhood of Teamsters, Chauffeurs,
    Warehousemen, and Helpers of America
25 Louisiana Avenue NW
Washington, DC 20001

General information about school bus driving is available from the following association:

National School Transportation Association
P.O. Box 2639
Springfield, VA 22152

General information on local transit bus driving is available from:

American Public Transit Association
1201 New York Avenue NW, Ste. 400
Washington, DC 20005

CHAPTER 26

OTHER UTILITIES

A hundred years ago, a town could provide clean water for its citizens with little difficulty, and removing sewage was simply a matter of putting in pipes to carry the waste away. Because of great growth in population and concentration of people, shortages of water, and massive areas that are affected by waste treatment, water works are now much more complicated; wastewater treatment plants are now much more important. As a result, utilities employ many technicians, such as wastewater treatment plant operators, as well as administrators and maintenance workers. In 1988, state and local government employment in sewerage, water supply, electric power, and gas supply was about 390,000, almost all of it at the local level.

WATER AND WASTEWATER TREATMENT PLANT OPERATORS

Part mechanic and part technician, these workers operate pumps, adjust valves, inspect pipes and other equipment, check gauges, and adjust controls. They take water samples and test them chemically or perform biological analyses. They make minor repairs to equipment. In larger plants, operators are more specialized, performing only one function; but in small plants, they do everything.

Water treatment plant operators usually work a 40-hour week; weekend and night hours are required, however, since most plants operate

120

around the clock. Operators move around in their work, climbing ladders and scrambling over pipes.

What you should bring to this occupation. Successful operators enjoy working with machinery. They should be agile enough to make their way around a plant and able to use wrenches and other hand tools. Chemical dust can cause trouble for operators with allergies.

A high school education is usually required. Applicants are tested for general intelligence, skill in elementary mathematics, and mechanical aptitude.

The rewards. Operators who enjoy working with machinery are most likely to find this job satisfying. The work environment can be a drawback because of noise and air pollution.

Advancement possibilities depend on the size of the plant. Larger plants usually offer more opportunities; the top jobs at larger plants, however, may require a college degree in engineering or science.

Water treatment plant operator is among the lower 30 percent of all occupations in terms of wages. In 1989, average wages were $21,300. Workers in larger plants, with more complicated jobs or with supervisory responsibilities, earn more. Operators receive the usual fringe benefits.

Where to find a job. About 76,000 water and sewage plant operators worked for local governments in 1989. They represent almost 90 percent of all the workers in this occupation. Water, sewerage, and pollution control departments are the most likely employers.

Slow growth is projected through 1995. New machinery may decrease the need for workers; however, jobs will become available due to turnover.

Where to learn more. Local employers are the best source of information about this occupation.

CHAPTER 27

WELFARE AND HUMAN SERVICES

Public welfare departments administer programs such as Aid to Families With Dependent Children, Food Stamps, and Medicaid. They may also provide social services like day-care, counseling, and home-maker services. In 1988, state and local government employment in public welfare was 417,000; state governments employed 193,000 people, counties 177,000, and cities 47,000. In addition to administrative and clerical workers—notably claims clerks—welfare departments employ thousands of social workers.

Social insurance administration and employment services have become government functions only in this century. The states administer unemployment insurance programs and worker's compensation programs and provide job counseling and job training. They also run the states' Job Services, which function like a state employment agency. Job Service employees interview applicants to determine their skills and interests, find employers with vacancies, and match the applicants with the openings.

SOCIAL WORKERS

Meeting some of the needs caused by poverty and disadvantage is the social worker's goal. Social caseworkers meet with individuals, families, or groups, try to identify what problems the people have, and suggest ways to solve them. Some temporary solutions are fairly simple.

For example, if a family has no money because the adults are unable to work, the social worker can arrange for welfare payments to be made. Many problems are much more complex—drug addiction, for example. In these cases, social workers may refer the clients to other specialists and programs. They are trained to recognize that many people with such severe problems may need more intensive and specialized care. Caseworkers are also trained in knowing how and where to refer people for special care, and in coordinating the services of different agencies. Most social workers are caseworkers—that is, they work directly with those in need—but some are administrators, teachers, or researchers.

Social workers may specialize in particular fields. About half of all social workers are in just three categories: mental health, child/youth, and medical/health. Similar work is performed by probation and parole officers, whose occupations are described in the chapter on correction departments.

Social workers usually have an 8-hour day, 5 days a week. Much of their time is spent in offices, but they may also visit clients.

What you should bring to this occupation. Successful social workers have the sensitivity to care for the needy and the maturity to face trying conditions. They make independent decisions at the same time that they accept the rules of their agency.

The usual educational requirement is a bachelor's degree in social work, psychology, or sociology. Some positions require a master of social work degree (MSW).

More than half the states require that social workers be licensed.

The rewards. Social workers have the satisfaction of helping people in need. Among the frustrations of the job are the relatively low wage—considering the education required—the difficulty of working with government agencies, and the apparent hopelessness of the situation: that needs are unlimited, and resources are limited.

Social workers may advance to supervisory positions or enter teaching. Further education may be necessary for advancement.

In 1988, the average salary was $22,000. Social workers receive the usual fringe benefits.

Where to find a job. About 185,000 social workers were employed by state and local governments in 1988; hospitals, about half of which are government run, employed an additional 48,000; and schools employed 21,000.

The major employers are departments of human resources, social services, mental health, housing, education, and correction.

This occupation is projected to grow about as fast as average through 1995. Many more positions will become available because of turnover, however. Turnover for social workers is relatively high, especially for an occupation that requires a college degree; this indicates that many employed social workers enter other occupations or leave the labor force entirely, rather than continue in their jobs.

Where to learn more. The following associations can provide further information:

National Association of Social Workers
7981 Eastern Avenue
Silver Spring, MD 20910

American Federation of State, County and Municipal Employees
1625 L Street NW
Washington, DC 20001

Council on Social Work Education
1600 Duke Street
Alexandria, VA 22314

CHAPTER 28

JOBS FOR TOMORROW

You would not be reading these words if you were not either preparing to train for a career *or* preparing to change careers. Your final decision may be affected by what you read in the coming pages. It is also possible that you will evaluate all the facts you can muster and still decide to enter an occupation that does not make anyone's "fastest growing" list. The decision, while yours alone, should be an informed one. If you want to spend your life in the wild as a forest ranger, then do it happily although armed in advance with the facts about salary, working conditions, and outlook for growth. If you yearn for a six-figure paycheck, by all means consider the outlook for those jobs that will provide one.

WHERE WILL THE JOBS COME FROM?

Most jobs through the year 2000 will result from replacement needs. Even jobs with slow growth potential will be available as people who hold them retire, return to school, assume household responsibilities, or, in the case of state and local government, leave for jobs in the private sector.

The jobs with the highest replacement levels are in those occupations that are large, have low pay and status, low training requirements, and a high proportion of young and part-time workers. The occupations with relatively few replacement openings are those with high pay and status, long training requirements, and a high proportion of full-time workers.

125

Other jobs will open up in large numbers in those categories that show faster than average growth. The *Occupational Outlook Handbook,* published by the U.S. Department of Labor, is the source of most of the information you will find in this chapter. Published every two years, it is a solid source of information about hundreds of jobs and includes sections on: the nature of the work, working conditions, number of people employed, training, other qualifications and chances for advancement, job outlook, earnings, related occupations, and sources of even more information. Please note that this is information for *all* jobs, both public and private. It will often tell you, however, how many of the total labor force is employed in the public sector. The *Handbook* can be purchased from the U.S. Department of Labor or from VGM Career Horizons, Lincolnwood, IL. It is also available in most public and school libraries.

FASTEST GROWING JOB MARKETS

The chart that follows will give you some idea where job opportunities look rosy in the coming years. It is important to remember two things as you look it over. First, look at both the percentage of increase expected *and* at the number of jobs. For example, the profession of *paralegal* tops the growth list in percentage (75%), but in numbers it shows 62,000. At the same time, computer system analysts show a 53 percent growth potential, but in real jobs you are looking at 214,000. The second thing to keep in mind is that this chart shows employment outlook in general, not in state and local government alone. It is, however, interesting to note that in the top ten jobs, only one, that of *travel agent,* is not to be found in governmental occupations.

We are reminded, once again, that public sector employment often mirrors the private sector, and movement between the two is not a difficult task. Some people leave the private sector for the greater security of the public sector, and some will leave the public sector for the possibility of faster or greater advancement they hope to find in the private sector.

Table 5:

Occupation	%Growth Expected	Numerical Growth	Estimated Total Employment– 1988
1 Paralegal	75	62,000	83,000
2 Medical Assistant	70	104,000	149,000
3 Radiologic technologist	66	87,000	132,000
4 Home health aide	63	207,000	327,000
5 Data processing equipment repairer	61	44,000	115,000
6 Medical secretary/ record technician	58	28,000	47,000
7 Physical therapist	57	39,000	68,000
8 Surgical technologist	56	20,000	35,000
9 Travel agent	54	77,000	142,000
10 Computer system analyst	53	214,000	402,000
11 Computer programmer	48	250,000	519,000
12 Health services manager	42	75,000	177,000

Source: U.S. Department of Labor

Other fast growing occupations are:

	(1988–2000) Numerical growth
• Registered nurse	613,000
• Correction officer	76,000
• Service sales representative	216,000
• Receptionist	331,000
• Licensed Practical Nurse	229,000

- Information clerk   441,000
- Nursing/psychiatric aide   405,000
- Guard   256,000

With the exception of service sales representative, you will see that these are, in large measure, jobs to be found in the public sector of employment.

TRENDS IN POPULATION TO YEAR 2000

Every other year the Bureau of Labor Statistics develops projections for the next 10-to-15-year period. Here are the trends most recently found.

- The U.S. population will grow more slowly.
- There will be fewer children and youths, with a growing population of middle-aged and older people—well into the twenty-first century.
- Minorities and immigrants will constitute a larger share of the total population.
- The West will continue to be the fastest growing area in the country (17%); the South will grow by 15%.

You can refine these trends even further by consulting with agencies in each state that keep similar statistics for their own state. A list of agencies, with addresses and telephone numbers, appears in a section titled "Sources of State and Local Job Outlook Information," in the *Occupational Outlook Handbook.*

LABOR FORCE TRENDS

- Population will increase from 121.7 million to 141.1 million.
- White non-Hispanic men will make up a smaller share of the labor force; women and minority group members will make up a larger share. African-Americans, Asians, and Hispanics will account for 33 percent of the labor force by the year 2000.

- Women will account for 47 percent of the work force—up from 41 percent in 1988.
- Workers between 25 and 54 years of age will make up 72 percent in 1988.
- Workers between 25 and 54 years of age will make up 72 percent of the labor force.
- Employment is expected to increase from 118 million to more than 136 million, or 15 percent.

As we shift from the Industrial Age to the Age of Information, from goods-producing to service-producing employment, we often question whether there will even *be* jobs for us in the future. The answer, as we can see, is that there will be jobs—more and more of them. As has been said many times, however, we may need to stay flexible, keep learning, and be more and more responsible for our futures. We will have to learn to be lifelong students; we will have to know where the jobs are and where the jobs *will be*. We also will have to know where and how to prepare for changing job markets. We need to remember that most of the jobs in the future will require a good bit of education. The jobs that used to go to high school dropouts and the minimally literate are the jobs that are disappearing. The job of the future must be filled by specially trained people who also are able to read and follow directions carefully. The new technology is, after all, only as good as the workers who are skilled in its use.

CHAPTER 29

LEARNING MORE ABOUT OCCUPATIONS AND JOBS

This book should make it obvious that governments offer a great range of employment opportunities. It is up to you to learn which ones suit you best. You will have to learn about your own state and neighboring states, your own local government and neighboring ones. You will have to decide which occupations appeal to you and then find out what qualifications these various governments demand and what benefits they offer. The sooner you do so, the better. You don't want to wait until the last minute only to find out that the examination you need to take was just offered and won't be given again for another year.

CHOOSING AND PREPARING FOR AN OCCUPATION

You should begin the process of choosing an occupation by analyzing yourself. Ask what you have—interests, skills, talents, physical conditions, work history, and education. Ask what you want: Money? Prestige? Adventure? To help others? To live in a certain place? To work on a team? Indoors? Part-time? Then explore careers, to find one that will most closely match what you want to do.

Career guidance and occupational information is provided in many books and magazines, several of which are listed in the appendix. Counseling to help you determine which occupations you are best prepared for may also be available. You'll also want to talk to people who actually have the kind of job you want. In many cases, they can point out things that books don't mention or make seem unimportant. One of the best ways to learn how much you like a job is to try it out through seasonal, part-time, or volunteer work.

Preparing for an occupation can be very expensive. Therefore, you want to be as certain as possible that the job is for you and that there will be a job for you. National outlook information is given throughout this book. For many people, however, the local outlook is much more important. It is also harder to determine. You can obtain some information from the state Job Service: the address of the office nearest you will be listed in the state government section of the telephone book. You can also contact potential employers and people now working in a field to ask how the future looks. Such a step is especially important before you commit yourself to an expensive educational program. Ask the school to give you the names of graduates now working in the occupation. Contact the graduates and ask if the schooling was worthwhile. Also contact their employers to learn if the particular school's program is highly thought of, or if it played no part in the decision to hire the graduate. You can also contact the Better Business Bureau to learn if there are any complaints about the school. A school that will not provide references—and one that promises you a job—should be treated with suspicion. For information on education and training programs, check the public library or school library. Talk to the librarians and gather as much information as you can before making a decision.

BOOKS AND MAGAZINES

The following list is a selection of books and magazines that contain career guidance and occupational information. The bibliographies in these books will lead you to many more publications.

CAREER GUIDANCE AND THE JOB HUNT

Coming Alive From Nine to Five, Betty Neville Michelozzi, Palo Alto, CA: Mayfield Publishing Co., 1988. Career planning, with exercises for self assessment.

How To Land a Better Job, Catherine S. Lott and Oscar C. Lott, Lincolnwood, IL: VGM Career Horizons, 1989. Covers everything from finding leads to negotiating salaries.

How To Write a Winning Resume, Deborah Perlmutter, Lincolnwood, IL: VGM Career Horizons, 1989. Filled with tips and examples.

What Color Is Your Parachute? A Practical Manual for Job-Hunters and Career-Changers, Richard N. Bolles, Berkeley, CA: Ten Speed Press, 1991. (New editions frequent.) Quite possibly the most frequently recommended guide to finding a career (not just a job).

Joyce Lain Kennedy's Career Book, Joyce Lain Kennedy, coauthored with Dr. Darryl Laramore, Lincolnwood, IL: VGM Career Horizons, 1992.

OCCUPATIONAL INFORMATION

Career World: The Continuing Guide to Careers, Highwood, IL: Curriculum Innovations (9 issues per year). Frequent articles on resumes and job hunting; many articles on occupations.

The Complete Guide to Public Employment, Ronald L. Krannich, Impact Publications, Woodbridge, VA, 1990.

Occupational Outlook Handbook, Washington, DC: U.S. Department of Labor (biennial). Considerable information on 250 or so occupations, including training requirements, salaries, outlook, and nature of the work.

Occupational Outlook Quarterly, Washington, DC: U.S. Department of Labor (quarterly). Complementary to the *Handbook,* the *Quarterly* includes material on occupational trends and patterns.

Chronicle of Occupational Briefs, Chronicle Guidance Publications, Inc. Moravia, NY. A series of over 400 regularly updated pamphlets each dealing with a specific occupation such as assessor and probation officer.

The Standard Periodical Directory, New York, NY: Oxbridge Communications, Incorporated (annual). A guide to more than 60,000 periodicals, thousands of which concern specific occupations.

INFORMATION ON STATE AND LOCAL GOVERNMENT

The Career Information Center: Public and Community Services, Vol. 11, Encino, CA: Glencoe Publishing Company, 1984. Descriptions of occupations often found in government agencies.

Careers in State and Local Government, John William Zehring, Garrett Park, MD: Garrett Park Press, 1980. A general guide book filled with sample position announcements, application forms, and sources of additional information.

Pay Rates in the Public Sector, Washington, DC: International Personnel Management Association (annual). Current salary information on 60 different occupations.

Public Employment, Washington, DC: U.S. Department of Commerce, Bureau of the Census (annual). Current data on employment by function.

Public Sector Jobs, P.0. Box 9, Baldwinsville, NY (biweekly).

The Book of States, Lexington, KY: The Council of State Governments (biennial). Current articles on every function of state government. *See below.*

The Municipal Year Book, Washington, DC: International City Management Association (annual). Current articles and directories of officials for thousands of cities; now includes directories of county officials.

The National Directory of State Agencies, compiled by N.D. Wright, J.
G. McCartney, and G.P. Allen, Washington, DC: Herner and Company,
Information Resources Press (biennial). Names and addresses.

Council of State Governments, Iron Works Pike, PO Box 11910,
Lexington, KY 40578.

APPENDIX B

ASSOCIATIONS

Many associations provide a wealth of information to job seekers. Three types of information will probably be most useful: career guidance material in either books or pamphlets; periodicals that contain position announcements, want ads, or articles about new developments in the field, and directories of members—which you can use to find local people to talk to about an occupation. Besides the associations listed elsewhere in this book, many other associations are listed in the *Encyclopedia of Associations,* an annual 3-volume publication, Gale Research Company, Detroit, MI 48226. Section 3 of the *Encyclopedia* lists associations in government and public administration; the other sections of the *Encyclopedia* list thousands of occupational associations. *Careers in State and Local Government* (listed above) also lists the names and addresses of many associations.

PERSONNEL DEPARTMENTS

STATES AND TERRITORIES

Alabama
Department of Personnel
402 Administrative Bldg.
64 North Union Street
Montgomery, AL 36130

Alaska
Division of Personnel and Labor Relations
Department of Administration
State Office Building, Pouch C
Juneau, AK 99811

Arizona
Personnel Division
Department of Administration
1831 West Jefferson Street
Phoenix, AZ 85007

Arkansas
Office of Personnel Management
Department of Finance and Administration
1509 W. 7th Street
P.O. Box 3278
Little Rock, AR 72203

California
Personnel Board
801 Capitol Mall
Box 94420
Sacramento, CA 94244–2010
Colorado
Department of Personnel
122 Centennial Building
1313 Sherman Street
Denver, CO 80203
Connecticut
Personnel Division
Department of Administrative Services
State Office Building
165 Capitol Avenue
Hartford, CT 06106
Delaware
State Personnel Office
Executive Office of the Governor
Townsend Building Federal Street
P.O. Box 1401
Dover, DE 19901
District of Columbia
Personnel Office
South Potomac Building, Room 306
613 G Street NW
Washington, DC 20001
Florida
Division of Personnel
Department of Administration
330 Carlton Building
Calhoun Street
Tallahassee, FL 32304

Georgia
Merit System of Personnel Administration
Floyd Memorial Building West Tower, Ste. 504
200 Piedmont Avenue SE
Atlanta, GA 30334
Hawaii
Department of Personnel Services
Keelikolani Building
830 Punchbowl Street
Honolulu, HI 96813
Idaho
Idaho Personnel Commission
State Office Building
700 West State Street
Boise, ID 83720
Illinois
Department of Personnel
503 William G. Stratton Office Building
401 South Spring Street
Springfield, IL 62706
Indiana
Personnel Division
Department of Administration
513 State Office Building
100 North Senate Avenue
Indianapolis, IN 46204
Iowa
Merit Employment Department
Grimes State Office Building
400 East 14th Street
Des Moines, IA 50319–0150
Kansas
Division of Personnel Services
Department of Administration
Landon State Office Building, Room 951–5
900 Jackson Street
Topeka, KS 66612

Kentucky
Department of Personnel
373 New Capitol Annex
Frankfort, KY 40601
Louisiana
Department of State Civil Service
Republic Tower
5700 Florida Boulevard
Box 94111–9111
Baton Rouge, LA 70804
Maine
Department of Personnel
214 State Office Building
Augusta, ME 04333
Maryland
Department of Personnel
State Office Building
301 West Preston Street
Baltimore, MD 21201
Massachusetts
Division of Personnel Administration
John W. McCormack State Office Building
One Ashburton Place
Boston, MA 02108
Michigan
Department of Civil Service
Lewis Cass Building
320 South Walnut Street
P.O. Box 30002
Lansing, MI 48909
Minnesota
Department of Personnel
Space Center Building
520 Lafayette Road
St. Paul, MN 55155

Mississippi
State Personnel Board
301 N. Lamar Street, Ste. 100
Jackson, MS 39201

Missouri
Division of Personnel
Office of Administration
Harry S. Truman State Office Building, Room 430
P.O. Box 388
Jefferson City, MO 65102

Montana
Personnel Division
Department of Administration
130 Sam W. Mitchell Building
205 Roberts Street
Helena, MT 59620

Nebraska
Department of Personnel
State Office Building
301 Centennial Mall, South
P.O. Box 94905
Lincoln, NE 68509–4905

Nevada
Personnel Division
Department of Administration
209 East Musser Street
Carson City, NV 89710

New Hampshaire
Personnel Department
1 State House Annex
Capitol Street
Concord, NH 03301

New Jersey
Department of Civil Service
Arnold Constable Building
215 East State Street
Trenton, NJ 08625

New Mexico
State Personnel Board
130 South Capitol Street
Santa Fe, NM 87503
New York
Department of Civil Service
One West Averill Harriman Office Building
Albany, NY 12239
North Carolina
Office of State Personnel
Department of Administration
Administration Building
116 West Jones Street
Raleigh, NC 27611
North Dakota
Central Personnel Division
Office of Management and Budget
State Capitol, 14th Floor
Bismarck, ND 58505
Ohio
Division of Personnel
Department of Administration Services
State Office Tower
30 East Broad Street
Columbus, OH 43266
Oklahoma
Office of Personnel Management
G-40 Jim Thorpe Office Building
2101 North Lincoln Boulevard
Oklahoma City, OK 73105
Oregon
Personnel and Labor Relations Division
155 Cottage Street NE
Salem, OR 97310

Pennsylvania
Bureau of Personnel
Office of the Governor
517 Finance Building
Harrisburg, PA 17120
Puerto Rico
Central Office for Personnel Administration
P.O. Box 8476
Fernandez Juncos Station
Santurce, PR 00910
Rhode Island
Division of Personnel Administration
Department of Administration
CIC Complex
289 Promenade Street
Providence, RI 02908
South Carolina
Division of Human Resources Management
Budget and Control Board
AT&T Building, Ste. 1016
1201 Main Street
P.O. Box 12547 Capitol Station
Columbia, SC 29211
South Dakota
Bureau of Personnel
Department of Executive Management
Public Safety Building
118 W. Capitol Avenue
Pierre, SD 57501
Tennessee
Department of Personnel
James K. Polk Office Building, 2nd Floor
Nashville, TN 37219–5185

Texas
Merit System Council
507 Broan Building
P.O. Box 1389
Austin, TX 78767
Utah
State Division of Personnel Management
State Office Building
Room 2222
Salt Lake City, UT 84114
Vermont
Department of Personnel
Agency of Administration
State Office Building
120 State Street
Montpelier, VT 05602
Virgin Islands
Division of Personnel
Office of the Governor
St. Thomas, VI 00801
Virginia
Department of Personnel and Training
James Monroe Bldg., 12th Floor
101 N. 14th Street
Richmond, VA 23219
Washington
Department of Personnel
600 South Franklin Street
P.O. Box 1789
Olympia, WA 98507
West Virginia
Civil Service System
B456 State Office Building 6
1900 Washington Street
East Charleston, WV 25305

Wisconsin
Division of Personnel
Department of Employment Relations
P.O. Box 7855
Madison, Wl 53707
Wyoming
Personnel Division
Department of Administration and Fiscal Control
Emerson Building
2001 Capitol Avenue
Cheyenne, WY 82002

THE TEN LARGEST CITIES

New York
City of New York
Department of Personnel
49 Thomas Street
New York, NY 10013
Los Angeles
Personnel Department
City Employment Office
111 East First Street
Los Angeles, CA 90012
Chicago
Department of Personnel
Room 1100
121 North Lasalle Street
Chicago, IL 60602
Philadelphia
Employment Application Center
127 City Hall
Philadelphia, PA 19107
(residents only)

Dallas
Civil Service
2014 Main Street
Dallas, TX 75201

San Diego
Personnel
202 C Street
San Diego, CA 92101

Phoenix
Personnel Department
Municipal Building
300 West Washington
Phoenix, AZ 85003

Baltimore
City of Baltimore
Civil Service Commission
111 North Calvert Street
Baltimore, MD 21202

Houston
City of Houston
Department of Personnel
P.O. Box 1562
Houston, TX 77251
(street address: 806 Main, 4th floor)

Detroit
Personnel
316 City-County Building
2 Woodward Street
Detroit, MI 48226

THE TEN LARGEST COUNTIES

Los Angeles
County of Los Angeles
Personnel Department
222 North Grand Avenue
Los Angeles, CA 90012

Dade
Metropolitan Dade County
Employment Relations Department
Employment Services Division
200 South Miami Avenue, Suite 240
Miami, FL 33130
Harris
Personnel
1 Clark Street
Room 834
Houston, TX 77020
Nassau
Nassau County Civil Service Commission
140 Old Country Road
Mineola, NY 11501
Suffolk
Civil Service
65 Jetson Lane
Central Islip, NY 11722
Erie
Personnel Department
95 Franklin Street
Buffalo, NY 14202
Santa Clara
Department of Personnel
70 West Hedding
San Jose, CA 95110
Orange
Department of Personnel
10 Civic Center Plaza
Santa Ana, CA 92701
Alameda
Civil Service Commission
Personnel Department
1212 Oak Street
Oakland, CA 94612

Cuyahoga
Cuyahoga County Board of County Commissioners
Personnel Department
1219 Ontario Street
Cleveland, OH 44113
San Diego
Office of Employee Services
County Administration Center
1600 Pacific Highway
Room 207
San Diego, CA 92101

THE TEN LARGEST SCHOOL DISTRICTS

New York
New York City Board of Education
Division of Personnel
65 Court Street
Brooklyn, NY 11201
Los Angeles
Los Angeles City Board of Education
450 North Grand Avenue
Los Angeles, CA 90012
(also see the telephone directory
under Los Angeles Board of Education)
Chicago
Teacher Personnel
OR
Service Personnel
1819 West Pershing
Chicago, IL 60609

Detroit
Detroit Public Schools
Teacher Employment Office
5057 Woodward Avenue
Room 440
Detroit, MI 48202
Houston
Houston Independent School District
3830 Richmond Avenue
Houston, TX 77027
Broward County
Broward County School District
1320 SW Fourth Street
Ft. Lauderdale, FL 33312
Dallas
Dallas Independent School District
3807 Ross Avenue
Dallas, TX 75204
Dade County
Dade County Public Schools
1410 NE Second Avenue
Miami, FL 33132
Philadelphia
Board of Education
Department of Personnel
21st and Race Streets
Philadelphia, PA 19103
Fairfax County
Fairfax County Public Schools
The Administration Center
10700 Page Avenue
Fairfax, VA 22030

VGM CAREER BOOKS

OPPORTUNITIES IN
*Available in both paperback and
hardbound editions*
Accounting
Acting
Advertising
Aerospace
Agriculture
Airline
Animal and Pet Care
Architecture
Automotive Service
Banking
Beauty Culture
Biological Sciences
Biotechnology
Book Publishing
Broadcasting
Building Construction Trades
Business Communication
Business Management
Cable Television
Carpentry
Chemical Engineering
Chemistry
Child Care
Chiropractic Health Care
Civil Engineering
Cleaning Service
Commercial Art and Graphic Design
Computer Aided Design and
  Computer Aided Mfg.
Computer Maintenance
Computer Science
Counseling & Development
Crafts
Culinary
Customer Service
Dance
Data Processing
Dental Care
Direct Marketing
Drafting
Electrical Trades
Electronic and Electrical Engineering
Electronics
Energy
Engineering
Engineering Technology
Environmental
Eye Care
Fashion
Fast Food
Federal Government
Film
Financial
Fire Protection Services
Fitness
Food Services
Foreign Language
Forestry
Gerontology
Government Service
Graphic Communications
Health and Medical
High Tech
Home Economics
Hospital Administration
Hotel & Motel Management
Human Resources Management
  Careers
Information Systems
Insurance
Interior Design
International Business
Journalism
Laser Technology
Law

Law Enforcement and Criminal Justice
Library and Information Science
Machine Trades
Magazine Publishing
Management
Marine & Maritime
Marketing
Materials Science
Mechanical Engineering
Medical Technology
Metalworking
Microelectronics
Military
Modeling
Music
Newspaper Publishing
Nursing
Nutrition
Occupational Therapy
Office Occupations
Opticianry
Optometry
Packaging Science
Paralegal Careers
Paramedical Careers
Part-time & Summer Jobs
Performing Arts
Petroleum
Pharmacy
Photography
Physical Therapy
Physician
Plastics
Plumbing & Pipe Fitting
Podiatric Medicine
Postal Service
Printing
Property Management
Psychiatry
Psychology
Public Health
Public Relations
Purchasing
Real Estate
Recreation and Leisure
Refrigeration and Air Conditioning
Religious Service
Restaurant
Retailing
Robotics
Sales
Sales & Marketing
Secretarial
Securities
Social Science
Social Work
Speech-Language Pathology
Sports & Athletics
Sports Medicine
State and Local Government
Teaching
Technical Communications
Telecommunications
Television and Video
Theatrical Design & Production
Transportation
Travel
Trucking
Veterinary Medicine
Visual Arts
Vocational and Technical
Warehousing
Waste Management
Welding
Word Processing
Writing
Your Own Service Business

CAREERS IN Accounting; Advertising;
Business; Communications; Computers;
Education; Engineering; Health Care;
High Tech; Law; Marketing; Medicine;
Science

CAREER DIRECTORIES
Careers Encyclopedia
Dictionary of Occupational Titles
Occupational Outlook Handbook

CAREER PLANNING
Admissions Guide to Selective
  Business Schools
Career Planning and Development for
  College Students and Recent
  Graduates
Careers Checklists
Careers for Animal Lovers
Careers for Bookworms
Careers for Culture Lovers
Careers for Foreign Language
  Aficionados
Careers for Good Samaritans
Careers for Gourmets
Careers for Nature Lovers
Careers for Numbers Crunchers
Careers for Sports Nuts
Careers for Travel Buffs
Guide to Basic Resume Writing
Handbook of Business and
  Management Careers
Handbook of Health Care Careers
Handbook of Scientific and
  Technical Careers
How to Change Your Career
How to Choose the Right Career
How to Get and Keep
  Your First Job
How to Get into the Right Law School
How to Get People to Do Things
  Your Way
How to Have a Winning Job Interview
How to Land a Better Job
How to Make the Right Career Moves
How to Market Your College Degree
How to Prepare a *Curriculum Vitae*
How to Prepare for College
How to Run Your Own Home Business
How to Succeed in Collge
How to Succeed in High School
How to Write a Winning Resume
Joyce Lain Kennedy's Career Book
Planning Your Career of Tomorrow
Planning Your College Education
Planning Your Military Career
Planning Your Young Child's
  Education
Resumes for Advertising Careers
Resumes for College Students & Recent
  Graduates
Resumes for Communications Careers
Resumes for Education Careers
Resumes for High School Graduates
Resumes for High Tech Careers
Resumes for Sales and Marketing Careers
Successful Interviewing for College
  Seniors

SURVIVAL GUIDES
Dropping Out or Hanging In
High School Survival Guide
College Survival Guide

VGM Career Horizons
a division of *NTC Publishing Group*
4255 West Touhy Avenue
Lincolnwood, Illinois 60646-1975